MEI structured mathematics

Commercial and Industrial Statistics

W. Gibson

Series Editor: Roger Porkess

MEI Structured Maths is supported by industry:
BNFL, Casio, GEC, Intercity, JCB, Lucas, The National Grid Company,
Sharp, Texas Instruments, Thorn EMI

Acknowledgements

The authors and publishers would like to thank The Met Office, the Controller of HMSO and The Office for National Statistics for kind permission to reproduce copyright material for this book.

The illustrations were drawn by Jeff Edwards Illustrations.

Cataloguing in Publication Data is available from the British Library

ISBN 0 340 658568

First published 1997
Impression number 10 9 8 7 6 5 4 3 2 1
Year 2003 2002 2001 2000 1999 1998 1997

Copyright © 1997 W. Gibson

Typeset by Alden, Oxford, Didcot and Northampton.
Printed in Great Britain for Hodder & Stoughton Educational, a division of Hodder Headline Plc, 338 Euston Road, London NW1 3BH by Scotprint Ltd, Musselburgh, Scotland.

MEI Structured Mathematics

Mathematics is not only a beautiful and exciting subject in its own right but also one that underpins many other branches of learning. It is consequently fundamental to the success of a modern economy.

MEI Structured Mathematics is designed to increase substantially the number of people taking the subject post-GCSE, by making it accessible, interesting and relevant to a wide range of students.

It is a credit accumulation scheme based on 45 hour components which may be taken individually or aggregated to give:

3 Components   AS Mathematics

6 Components   A Level Mathematics

9 Components   A Level Mathematics + AS Further Mathematics

12 Components A Level Mathematics + A Level Further Mathematics

Components may alternatively be combined to give other A or AS certifications (in Statistics, for example) or they may be used to obtain credit towards other types of qualification.

The course is examined by the Oxford and Cambridge Examinations and Assessment Council, with examinations held in January and June each year.

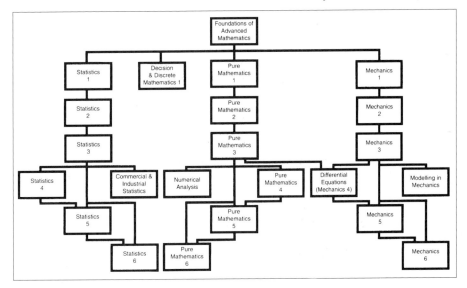

This is one of the series of books written to support the course. Its position within the whole scheme can be seen in the diagram above.

Mathematics in Education and Industry is a curriculum development body which aims to promote the links between Education and Industry in Mathematics at secondary school level, and to produce relevant examination and teaching syllabuses and support material. Since its foundation in the 1960s, MEI has provided syllabuses for GCSE (or O Level), Additional Mathematics and A Level.

For more information about MEI Structured Mathematics or other syllabuses and materials, write to MEI Office, 11 Market Place, Bradford-on-Avon, BA15 1LL.

Introduction

Of making many books there is no end, and much study is a weariness of the flesh.

King Solomon

Commercial and Industrial Statistics is one of a series of books written for the components in the MEI Structured Mathematics scheme but it may also be used independently of the scheme. The book assumes knowledge of the modules Pure Mathematics 1, 2 and 3 and Statistics 1, 2 and 3 which together would constitute an A-level.

The book gives an introduction to data collection by surveys and experiments, statistical methods for quality control, the analysis of time series and forecasting. It shows how the theory learnt in the preceding modules may be applied in the world of commerce and industry.

Most of the examples in the book contain data based on those supplied by real organisations, but in many cases the data have been modified in order to illustrate particular points. Unless a source is given, you can assume that data sets are *realistic* but not *real*.

If you could provide one or more data sets which could be used in conjunction with this book, I should be delighted to receive them via the MEI office. Hopefully a set of resources will be assembled and made generally available.

Finally I should like to express my gratitude to the many people who have helped me with this book. There are many people in commerce and industry who have spoken with me, explained how they use statistics and/or provided me with material for examples. The list includes people in national and international firms – such as Glaxo Wellcome, ICI and British Gas – and those in local firms – such as Cramlington Textiles, Cascade (Hydraulics) and North East Press. I am grateful to my friends and colleagues for the encouragement and the practical help which they have provided, and to the reviewers for their helpful comments and criticisms.

W. Gibson

Contents

Design of surveys

Many people use statistics rather like a drunken man uses a lamp post: more for support than for illumination.

An opinion poll shows that the Labour Party has 43% of the votes and the Conservative Party has 39%. Does this mean that the Labour Party will win the next election?

Why might the results of the election differ from those of the opinion poll?

If you were given the job of predicting the result of the next election, how would you go about it? How would financial constraints influence your choice of strategy?

Data collection: definition of terms

An opinion poll is an example of a survey. The aim of a survey is to collect information from a sample of a *population,* and to use this to try to say something about the population as a whole. The population, sometimes called the *target* or *parent* population, may be made up of people, animals, plants or inanimate objects.

The intention of a survey is not to alter the characteristics or opinions of the population. For example, the purpose of a political opinion poll is to find out how people in the sample intend to vote, and to use that information to estimate the voting intentions of the whole of the population. The opinion poll does not aim to cause people to vote in any particular way. (It is possible, of course, that asking people about their voting intentions might make them think about the issue, and so change them from a non-voter into a voter.)

A survey that obtains information from the whole of the population of interest is called a census. A firm developing a new staff restaurant for its employees could use a census to find out about the food preferences of all of its current employees. A census provides complete information, which usually makes it relatively easy to draw conclusions. Very often, though, a census is either impractical or impossible, so a sample is used instead.

When conducting a survey the size of the sample, the variability of the parent population and the way in which you select the sample will all influence the reliability of any conclusions you draw about the parent population. However, if you object in principle to the use of a sample to draw conclusions about a parent population, you should make the same objection if you need to have a blood test and the doctor only takes a sample!

Choosing a sample and then obtaining information from it is time-consuming and usually costly. It is important to choose your sample in such a way as to give valid information about the population while keeping the sample size (and hence the cost in time and/or money) as low as possible. Surveys which use too large a sample are clearly wasteful, but surveys which use too small a sample may also turn out to be wasteful as they may not produce sufficiently precise or reliable information.

NOTE

The terms 'survey' and 'experiment' are often confused. In an experiment the values of one, or more, of the variables are actually chosen by the experimenter. For example, if the yield of a chemical process were thought to depend upon the temperature at which the process operates you could investigate this by running the process at suitable temperatures and measuring the yields. The design and analysis of experiments is dealt with in Chapters 3 and 4.

Initial planning

It is not unknown for a researcher to ask a statistician how to analyse a pile of carefully collected data and to be told that the best thing would be to throw it away and start again! Although this may sound almost unbelievable, there are many accounts of it having happened and, in some cases, the money wasted was reckoned in the tens of thousands of pounds.

In order to avoid such waste, you need to plan surveys carefully. Before undertaking a survey, you should consider the following key questions.

* **What do you actually want to know?**
  This question sounds easy to answer but sometimes it is very difficult. Often you want to know about totals or proportions: in an opinion poll you are interested in the proportion of voters who intend voting for each of the political parties. A library might be interested in estimating the total number of its books which need repairing and the time and expense which would be involved. However, if you wish to find out whether the standard of living has risen during the last decade, it is more difficult to decide what information you need to collect in order to answer the question.

* **How are you going to choose the sample?**
  Your sample must be representative of the parent population in which you are interested. To ensure this, you must choose the sample by some random method. This means that the selection of the sample should be by objective means rather than by the direct choice of some person. (Methods of random sampling are covered on pages 9–15.)

* **What are you going to measure?**
  Usually you measure the thing in which you are interested. For example, in an opinion poll, you simply record the party for which the voters say they intend voting. If you want to estimate the total volume of water used by the inhabitants of a town, you measure the amount of water used by the families in a sample.

Sometimes it is not possible to measure the item of interest directly, and so you measure one or more related variables. For example, to estimate the total volume of wood in a section of forest (without felling all of the trees) you could measure the height and the diameter of a sample of the trees and use these figures to estimate the volume.

- **How large a sample should you take?**
- **What will be the precision of your results?**

The answers to these two questions are linked. Usually, the greater the precision required, the larger the sample that must be taken. Also, the greater the variability in the population, the larger the sample required to gain the necessary precision. These questions will be addressed in more detail in the next chapter.

- **How will you analyse the results?**

This question is linked with all of the others. It needs to be answered before the data are collected, as it affects the answers to all of the other questions. If you do not answer it, you may find that your data are inappropriate, inadequate or insufficient for the purpose of the survey. The analysis that you plan to do may simply involve tables and charts, or it may involve hypothesis tests and confidence intervals.

Deciding in advance how to analyse the data does not prevent you from using extra or alternative methods when you come to the analysis. You need to be free to respond to the data, but you also need to be sure that the data will be adequate (and in the correct form) for some kind of analysis.

For Discussion

Try to answer the key questions for each of the situations described below.

1. A firm which produces light bulbs needs to say how long they will last.
2. A regional water company needs to know how much water an average family uses each day.
3. A travel agent wants to find out how satisfied its customers were with the holidays they had booked through the firm.

Exercise 1A

1. A software house wishes to know how much its customers use the manuals provided with the software, and how helpful they find them. They have lists of registered users of their ten major software packages for the last five years. The list consists of about ten thousand customers. State briefly what the company should do to obtain this information using a survey, remembering that both time and money are limited.

2. The manager of a building society branch wants to know how satisfied the customers are with the service they receive. She assumes that there will be a difference between the following categories of customer.
   - Those who have only a mortgage account.
   - Those who have only a savings account.
   - Those who have both types of account.

Lists of all of the customers and their accounts are available. How should the manager obtain the information she requires?

3. A factory discharges some of its waste products into a nearby river. Production in the factory, and hence of the waste, starts at 0800 hours and ends at 1700 hours. The pattern of work is similar each day. To monitor the waste levels, water samples are taken from a fixed point 50 m downstream from the point of discharge. Because of the time and cost involved in taking and analysing the samples, only 5 samples are taken each week.

(i) Explain why it would be inappropriate to take one sample each day at 10:00 hours.

(ii) Devise a simple sampling scheme which the factory could use, still taking only 5 samples per week.

Methods of collecting information

The main methods of collecting information from a sample are:
- personal interview
- telephone interview
- postal questionnaire
- direct observation.

One large market research organisation said recently that 54% of its data collection was by personal interview, 16% by telephone interview and 9% by self-completion/postal questionnaire. Other methods used included noting responses in group discussions.

Personal interviews are the best way of obtaining accurate information from all of the people in a sample. A good interviewer can clarify the questions where necessary, and encourage the interviewee to respond carefully and honestly. However, training and employing good interviewers is costly, and if interviewees are to be visited at their homes the travel and time costs for the interviewer(s) can be very large.

Telephone interviews save money on travel costs, but the lack of face-to-face contact may make the interviewee less likely to answer some questions. Also, of course, people cannot be in the sample if they do not have a telephone. For some surveys, such as one on means-tested benefits, it could be very important to include poorer families and so a telephone survey might not be appropriate. If the telephone directory is used as the basis for producing the sampling frame for a telephone survey, people who have chosen to be ex-directory will be excluded.

Postal surveys do not require trained interviewers and are therefore relatively cheap. However, a response rate of only 30% is not uncommon. This could introduce considerable bias into the sample. For example, in a survey about the difficulty of understanding and filling in income tax forms, the non-respondents might be those who find it difficult to fill in any type of form and hence their view would be under-represented in the survey. In some cases follow-up letters are sent to non-respondents, or an interviewer may be used for follow-up.

Design of surveys

CIS

Direct observation can be a very convenient way of collecting information where it is possible. To estimate the proportion of cars that do not have a valid road fund licence, the vehicle licensing authority could send employees to count how many of the cars in some large car parks have valid licences. This assumes that the car parks contain a representative sample of all cars.

Remote monitoring, an extension of direct observation, is made possible by electronic technology. One well-known example of this is the collection of viewing figures by TV companies. The members of the chosen sample of viewers are provided with monitors linked to their televisions, and details of the programmes that they have watched can be collected directly from the monitors via a telephone line. In this way, very accurate information can be obtained very quickly. The information is used by the television companies in planning future programme schedules, and by advertisers in deciding which time slots to use.

For Discussion

Which method of data collection would you use in the following situations? Think about the kind of information which you wish to obtain, and the cost of obtaining it.

1. A candidate in a local election wishes to have an estimate of the number of people who intend voting for her.

2. The manager of a fitness centre wants to know about the amount of exercise currently taken by people on four nearby housing estates. He also needs information on whether they consider themselves fit or unfit, and underweight, overweight or about right.

3. A railway authority wants to estimate the proportion of pedestrians who start to cross level crossings when the warning lights are already flashing.

Non-response

The problem of non-response is an important one whichever method of data collection is used. The non-response could be due to the person being out or busy when the interviewer visited or telephoned. In this case some carefully planned follow-up work would probably produce an adequate response-rate. In the case of postal questionnaires, a random sample of the non-respondents is sometimes visited by an interviewer and asked to complete the questionnaire in order to try to see if the people who didn't answer the postal questionnaire differ in any significant way from those who did.

Alternatively, interviewees may be unwilling to answer the questions because of embarrassment or resentment. For example, many people would be sensitive about answering questions on their personal finances, particularly if they thought that the tax office might learn of their responses. A good interview technique can often overcome some of the barriers, and there are ways of guaranteeing confidentiality for respondents: you will meet these in Chapter 2.

Questionnaire design

It is not easy to design a good questionnaire. Care must be taken to pose the questions clearly and in a neutral manner. In some contexts, even the order of the questions can affect people's responses to them. A poorly designed questionnaire can produce inadequate, ambiguous or distorted results.

The best way to check a questionnaire is to use a *pilot survey*. You ask a cross section of the parent population to answer the questions in the same way as you intend for the actual survey. This will identify most of the problems in its design and avoid the waste of time and money that results from using a defective questionnaire. For example, if the respondent is asked to tick one or more options in response to a question, the pilot survey may indicate that extra options are needed. This would be obvious from frequent ticking of the option 'Other: Please specify'.

The language used in questionnaires is very important as it can influence the respondent. In a dispute over pay within a company, the union might test employee opinion with questions including words such as 'mean' and 'miserly', whereas the management might tend to use words like 'sensible' and 'appropriate'. The two sides might end up with very different impressions of the employees' mood. To get an accurate view, neutral language should be used.

A travel firm wishing to know its customers' views about a particular holiday might send a postal questionnaire to the people who had been on that holiday. If the questionnaire just asked for comments, the firm might find it hard to evaluate the responses (is Ms Jolley's 'fabulous' the same as Mr Grump's 'not bad'?). To minimise this problem, they could offer a range of responses and ask respondents to tick one. Possible ranges are:

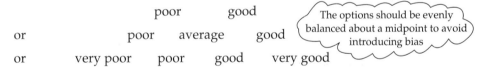

	poor		good	
or		poor	average	good
or	very poor	poor	good	very good

The options should be evenly balanced about a midpoint to avoid introducing bias

Alternatively, respondents could be offered a numerical scale ranging for example from 1 to 5. They could be told that '1' represented very poor and that '5' represented very good. Even then, the responses may depend on whether the options went from 'good' to 'poor' or from 'poor' to 'good'.

The order in which you pose questions can influence people's responses. A questionnaire used in the USA prior to the overturning of the Communist government in the then Soviet Union contained the following two questions.

A: *Do you think that the United States should let Communist newspaper reporters from other countries come in here and send back to their papers the news as they see it?*

B: *Do you think that a Communist country like Russia should let American reporters come in and send back to America the news as they see it?*

For Discussion

1. What do you think would be the effect of asking these questions in reverse order?

2. What do you think would happen if the two questions were on separate pages of the questionnaire, so that respondents had forgotten the first question when answering the second?

Sometimes you might include the option 'don't know', or 'I have no opinion on this matter', but often it is worth trying to persuade the interviewee to make a definite choice.

The number of questions should not be too large, because people might simply lose interest or be too busy to answer all of the questions. Some postal questionnaires offer rewards, such as free samples of products, to people who respond. Alternatively, the names of respondents may be entered in a prize draw.

Most survey data will be analysed by computer and so they need to be in a form that can be coded. For example 'no' and 'yes' can be coded as zero and 1. However, this means that the questions which are asked have to be *closed questions* – they only allow a small number of possible responses. Some respondents might find this too restrictive, so questionnaires often end with an optional *open question*, which allows the respondents to add comments on issues that they feel haven't been covered.

Activity

1. In a large electronics factory, all of the workers use the same canteen facilities for lunch. Workers pay a standard price for a 3-course meal. Currently the menu consists of
    *   soup of the day
    *   three choices of main course, one of which is vegetarian
    *   three choices of dessert, one of which is fruit.

    The canteen supervisor wants to know whether the employees are satisfied with the current options, or whether one extra option should be available for one or more of the courses. Extra options would require extra work and extra staff, and this would mean that the price of the meal would have to rise. It is estimated that offering an extra option in the first course would add 10% to the current price of the meal, and offering an extra option in the second and third courses would add 20% and 15%, respectively. Design a questionnaire to be given to a sample of the employees to help the canteen supervisor to make the decision.

2. Which faults can you identify in the following questions in a questionnaire designed to find out about people's opinions on the different political parties?
    (i) *The Green Party is much better than the other parties, isn't it?*
    (ii) *Do you think that Labour is better than the Conservatives?*

1

Activity (Continued)

    (ii) *You don't vote for the Liberal Democrats, do you?*
    (iv) *What do you think of the current government?*

Choosing a sample

The vital importance of using samples that are randomly chosen was not really appreciated until quite recently. However, it can be shown, using simple experiments, that people are not good at choosing representative samples, and that random methods always tend to be better in the long run. If you choose a sample by a subjective method, you will almost always introduce some bias. Of course, in any particular instance, you might choose a sample that turns out to give a better result than a random sample. However, this will not happen consistently, and random samples are much more reliable. The other major advantage of using a random method is that it allows you to estimate the precision of any estimates you make based on the sample data. This is covered in Chapter 2.

One obvious way of choosing a random sample is to put a piece of paper corresponding to each element of the parent population into a hat, then close your eyes and draw out pieces of paper one-by-one until you have the required sample size. This produces what is called a *simple random sample*. In practice it is more usual to use random number tables, or the random number generator on a calculator or computer rather than papers in a hat, but the principle is the same.

Simple random sampling is often the best sampling method to use. It is the method with which other methods are compared. However, in some situations modified sampling methods are more practical.

There are three main modifications of simple random sampling: *systematic sampling, stratified sampling* and *cluster sampling*. You will meet these later in this chapter, but first we shall look in more detail at simple random sampling.

Simple random sample

A *simple random sample* of size n is obtained by a procedure in which each set of n elements of the population has the same chance of being chosen. In order to select a simple random sample you need a sampling frame, a list of all of the members of the parent population. Usually, each element in the list is given a number, starting at 1. You then select elements for the sample using random number tables or the random number generator on a calculator or computer.

Suppose that you need to select a sample of 15 houses from a numbered list of 483 houses. Using random number tables, you choose a random starting position and take the digits in groups of three. If the first set of three digits is 247, you put house number 247 from the list into your sample. If the next number is 832, you ignore it because it does not correspond to a house in the list. You continue in this manner until you have a sample of 15 houses. (If any number occurs more than once, you still only include it once in the sample.)

In some circumstances, you might choose to assign random numbers in a less wasteful manner. For example, you could subtract 500 from any random numbers above 500, so instead of discarding 832 you would choose house (832 − 500) = 332. Whether this is worthwhile depends upon the sample size and the method being used to link the numbers to the elements in the sampling frame.

When using a random number generator on a calculator, you use the same procedure. If the calculator only provides three digits and you need five, you can generate two sets of three digits and discard the last digit.

Activity

Using the random numbers below, which items would you choose from a numbered list of the 17 841 inhabitants of a town if you want a random sample of size 10? Start with the top left random number and work along each row in order.

```
54 66 35 88 98 91 45 92 12 47 12 16 71 83 94 22 44 57 43 43
45 32 26 37 19 89 27 02 77 14 85 98 46 56 50 71 07 65 33 63
51 63 71 95 36 36 17 77 53 40 25 95 65 04 59 80 16 59 21 43
91 55 88 14 82 48 48 94 38 34 60 87 82 35 35 45 45 08 44 37
```

Simple random samples are the easiest to analyse, but they do have drawbacks in certain situations. You will tend to use an alternative sampling method when one or more of the following conditions apply:
- it would be extremely tedious to select the sample
- there is some clear structure in the parent population
- it is impossible, or extremely difficult, to produce a sampling frame.

Systematic sample

For Discussion

How would you go about choosing a random sample of size 1000 from the alphabetical listing in your local area telephone directory? How could the procedure be speeded up?

If you are selecting a fairly large sample from a large sampling frame, the process of generating random numbers and then finding the corresponding elements of the population can be very time-consuming and error-prone. It would be very laborious to find the 5438th name in the telephone directory. Even if the items in the sampling frame are numbered, large samples take time to select. If the sampling frame is on a computer database, life is much easier.

An alternative approach is to use a *systematic sample*. To select 1 element in 12 of the population, you choose a random number between 1 and 12 (using random number tables or generators) and then put this and every 12th element after it into the sample. Selecting items sequentially in this way from the sampling frame is much easier and quicker than selecting items in random order. Provided that the population is not in some order that depends on the characteristic in which you are interested, systematic sampling is equivalent to simple random sampling. The analysis of systematic samples is therefore the same as for simple random samples. If the elements in the sampling frame are ordered according to the item in which you are interested, systematic sampling is actually better than using a simple random sample as it guarantees that you cover almost the whole range of values.

If, however, the sampling frame contains periodic data such as monthly mean temperatures, it could be very misleading to use systematic sampling. This would certainly be the case if a sample of size 1 in 12 or 1 in 6 were to be chosen, since this would select the same month (or two months) for each year. Not many people would make this mistake, but the same sort of error could occur in circumstances where it was not so obvious.

A *transect* is a form of systematic sampling often used by biologists. If you were interested in the level of potassium in the soil in a particular area, you might choose at random a line that crossed the area, choose a starting point on the line at random, and take measurements at 10 m intervals. If you were investigating the moisture level in a field you could use another form of systematic sampling. You could divide the field into an appropriate number of square plots, then choose a point at random within one plot and take samples from the equivalent point in each of the plots.

Stratified sample

A local council is considering giving grants to enable people to increase loft insulation to the current recommended thickness. They want to estimate the cost of the scheme. One way to do this is to select a simple random sample of the dwellings in their area and find out the cost of increasing the loft insulation, where necessary, in these dwellings. However, this would ignore the obvious differences which exist between types of dwelling. Recently-built homes would tend to have the recommended thickness of insulation. Lower flats would not have a loft to insulate.

It would be more effective in this situation to take a random sample of each type of dwelling. If the council could assume that the dwellings of each type would have similar levels of insulation, the samples need not be large in order to obtain a reasonably precise estimate. This method would also avoid the possibility of the simple random sample consisting entirely of dwellings of only one type.

In situations like the above, where there are clear *strata* (plural) in the population, it is reasonable to select a simple random sample from each *stratum* (singular). This is called *stratified sampling*. Stratified sampling works best when there are large differences between the strata, but relatively small differences within the strata. If the differences within the strata are quite small, only a small sample is required in order to obtain accurate information about each stratum. The data may then be combined to provide information about the population as a whole. If simple random sampling had been used, a large sample would have been needed because of the large overall variability in the population.

If you know the exact (or approximate) size of each of the strata, it is usual to select a sample which is proportional to the size of the stratum. This is called *proportional allocation*.

If you have some extra information about the strata, such as the cost of information collection within each of the strata, or the amount of variability within each of the strata, you can take these into account in your choice of sample sizes. In a stratum which has a lot of variability, you require a larger sample to provide estimates of a specified precision. If you have a fixed overall budget, you might choose to take smaller samples from strata in which it is expensive to collect information. It is usually best to select sample sizes which are proportional to the size of the stratum, proportional to the standard deviation of the variable of interest within the stratum and inversely proportional to the square root of the cost of obtaining information from each item selected in the sample:

$$\text{sample size} \propto \frac{\text{stratum size} \times \text{standard deviation}}{\sqrt{\text{Cost per item}}}.$$

> If you know how the cost of collecting information varies between the strata, including this in the formula ensures that you obtain the maximum information for your money

For Discussion

For each of the following situations say whether you would be able to select a simple random sample and whether you would prefer to use some other method, which you should describe briefly.

1. You wish to use a sample to predict the outcome of an imminent national election.
2. You wish to predict the cost of repairing damaged books in a library. You suspect that the condition of a book will tend to depend upon its age, the number of times it has been issued, whether it is fiction or non-fiction and whether it is hardback or paperback. All of this information is available on the computer records.
3. As the manager of a large conifer plantation, you need to estimate the volume of timber which could be obtained by felling certain sections of the plantation. You are currently interested in the trees which are five years old. These were planted in 400 groups, each consisting of 100 trees.

Exercise 1B

1. A market research firm is asked to gauge attitudes to a proposed new wind farm development. The residents who could be affected fall into two basic categories: farmers and non-farmers. Because of the greater distances involved, it will be about twice as expensive to visit the farmers as the non-farmers. There are about 10 non-farmers to each farmer, and nothing is known about the variability in the expected responses. The market researcher is willing to interview about 300 people in total. How many of these should be farmers?

2. A supermarket wishes to estimate the average amount spent monthly on food by families in its locality.

   The people using the supermarket come mainly from 3 housing areas (A, B and C) and a large rural area. The housing areas have quite different characters and inhabitants, so the amounts spent on food, the variability in these amounts and the costs of obtaining the information will also differ. The organisation has undertaken similar surveys in other regions, and so initial esitmates of the likely results are based on that information. These are in the table below. Clearly the values might not apply exactly to the area in question, but they do provide a reasonable starting point.

Area	A	B	C	Rural
Population	30 000	20 000	15 000	5 000
Estimated average monthly spend	£125	£250	£375	£150
Estimated standard deviation	£10	£20	£40	£20
Cost per household of obtaining the information	£2	£2	£4	£6

A budget of £2000 has been allocated for data collection. How many households should be sampled from each of the four areas?

Cluster sample

The owner of a large forest asks you to estimate the total amount of timber in the forest. You know that there is considerable variability throughout the forest, but there is no reason to suppose that one section of the forest is substantially different from any other section.

In this situation, you could choose a simple random sample by using grid references on a map, but this would be extremely tedious and time consuming. It would also be very difficult to identify on the ground the trees that had been chosen on the map. Another alternative might be to choose a line through the forest at random (a transect), and to inspect each tree within a metre of the line. However, this too would be very tedious and difficult to implement.

Suppose instead that the forest is divided into fairly small sections, and that there is no reason to assume that the trees in one section are any different from those in another section. Stratified random sampling would not be appropriate, since the sections do not fulfil the conditions required, namely that the trees within a section are similar and that the sections differ considerably from each other.

The appropriate method here is *cluster sampling*. The first stage is to select a simple random sample of the sections of the forest – the *clusters*. The second stage is to extract the relevant information from all of the trees in each cluster (or from a simple random sample if there are too many trees in each section). If the clusters are of different sizes, it would be better to make the probability of selecting a particular cluster proportional to its size. In this case, that would mean making the probability of selecting a particular cluster proportional to its area.

For Discussion

How could you arrange for the probability of selecting a particular cluster to be proportional to its area?

The advantage of cluster sampling in this situation is that it reduces the time taken to collect the data. Since all of the elements in the cluster are close together it is relatively easy to collect the information. Using cluster sampling means that either the time and effort are reduced, or a larger sample can be obtained for the same expenditure of time and effort.

To undertake cluster sampling you require a sampling frame of all of the clusters, then a sampling frame for the elements of the selected clusters. You do not need to list the whole population. In a large-scale project this immediately results in a major saving of time and money. Since the elements within a cluster are almost always close together physically, there is usually a substantial saving of time in the collection of the information too.

The ideal time to use cluster sampling is when you have a relatively large number of clusters which are almost identical to each other. In this case, you need only a small number of clusters, as they will be good representatives of the others. If there are too many elements within a cluster for you to take information from all of them, you choose a sample within each cluster of a size that will give the required precision for the estimate you are making (see Chapter 2). Thus, the variation within each cluster can be relatively large, whereas the variability between the clusters should be relatively small. This is the opposite of the requirement for stratified samples.

Sometimes you might use cluster sampling (perhaps because of a lack of a sampling frame for the whole population) when you have reason to believe that the elements within a cluster will tend to be similar to each other, and not therefore representative of the population as a whole. This could occur with residents in small blocks of flats, or with teams of employees within an organisation, because of the interaction between the people. It could also occur if you were interested in trees within a forest affected by a disease if the disease actually spread from tree to tree. In statistical terms, the problem is that the values of the item of interest in the elements within a cluster are not independent. There is some correlation between the elements. In this situation you need to select a larger number of clusters in order to try to obtain information about the whole range of values in the population.

Note that this still differs from stratified sampling since you do not know in advance how the clusters will differ from each other.

Exercise 1C

1. A national chain of about 100 tyre and exhaust centres requires information about the mean time taken to fit a new exhaust to a particular popular model of car. Only one person is available to do the survey and he has only one week in which to do the work. Prepare a plan to be put to senior management suggesting a suitable strategy.

2. A large insurance company is concerned about the level of security at the homes of its clients and is considering offering new incentives to persuade people to fit suitable security measures. The company has 4 categories of risk, based on postcodes and past experience. A representative of the company is to visit 200 of the clients in the Greater Manchester area and assess their properties. Write a note for senior management suggesting how the sample should be chosen, giving a brief justification of your suggestion.

3. A water company wishes to estimate the amount of water used by households in its region over a year. To do this it proposes fitting water meters in 50 homes. The company has details of the number of people and the number of rooms in the households to which it supplies water. Write a brief plan suggesting how the sample should be chosen.

Other methods

Sometimes, for reasons of cost, convenience or practicality, the above methods are not employed. It is often very difficult to obtain a sampling frame from which to select a sample, and this makes it impracticable to use the methods described above. It would be very difficult, for example, to produce a sampling frame for all of the people who shop at a large shopping complex. You will often see interviewers on high streets or in shopping complexes. In most cases they are using *quota sampling* or *opportunity sampling*.

Quota sampling. A Newcastle travel company is considering offering a new range of cheap coach holidays to the Czech and Slovak Republics, Poland, Bulgaria and Hungary. It sends an interviewer to the city's main shopping complex to obtain information about the views of local people on the holidays and the proposed prices. The interviewer is told to interview 10 males and 10 females in each of the age groups 15–24, 25–34, 35–44, 45–54, 55–64 and 65 or over. This is an example of quota sampling, which is similar to stratified sampling, in that the interviewer is told to interview a certain number of people within several categories, or strata. In this case, the sample is stratified by age and sex. However, the interviewer is not selecting the sample from a sampling frame by some random method. Instead, she is making a subjective choice from the people who happen to be available at the time.

Opportunity sampling. The travel company mentioned above may alternatively tell the interviewer to select about 100 people and find their views on the proposed holidays and prices. This is called opportunity sampling, and it is similar to simple random sampling, in that the interviewer simply interviews a specified (minimum) number of people. It is also similar to quota sampling, but without strata. There is no sampling frame and no random selection; the interviewer simply chooses from the people who are available.

Both quota sampling and opportunity sampling may be used for other kinds of data collecting too. For example, an industrial chemist wishing to estimate the average size and the variability of the size of particles in a reagent would find it extremely difficult to produce a sampling frame of the particles in order to choose a random sample. She might use one of these sampling methods instead.

The two main problems with quota and opportunity sampling methods are
- there is no guarantee that the sample is representative of the parent population
- the choice of interviewee is usually left to the subjective choice of the interviewer.

Exercise 1D

1. (i) (a) Define what is meant by *simple random sampling*.
   (b) A simple random sample of size 20 is required from a population of size 100. The members of the population are labelled 00, 01, 02, ..., 98, 99. Use the following random digits to draw such a sample.

   Random digits:

   4 3 6 8 8 1 0 6 1 1 8 8 2 6 3 7 6 8 0 9
   8 1 2 3 7 7 1 6 4 4 3 7 1 4 7 4 3 9 1 2
   0 2 6 4 0 5 4 1 9 3 2 4 7 5 1 6 4 7 5 0

(ii) (a) Define what is meant by *systematic sampling* and state briefly its advantages and disadvantages.
   (b) Draw a systematic sample of size 20 from the population specified in part (i)(b), making clear how you have done so.

(iii) Define what is meant by *stratified sampling*. Describe a situation in which this might be more useful than simple random sampling, and explain why.

(iv) Describe how *quota sampling* is carried out. What are the advantages and disadvantages of this method of sampling?

KEY POINTS

When you have worked through this chapter you should
- understand the meaning of the technical terms *survey, census, sample, sampling frame, parent or target population, bias, pilot survey* and *proportional allocation*;
- know the advantages and disadvantages of the following sampling methods and when they should be used:
    - simple random sample
    - systematic sample
    - stratified sample
    - cluster sample
    - opportunity sample
    - quota sample.

Analysis of surveys

Statistics is a subject which stands on two legs: one is data collection and analysis, and the other is probability.

A referendum is to be conducted in which the electors are required to vote 'yes' or 'no' on a single issue. In an opinion poll prior to the referendum, a sample of 1000 electors are asked which way they intend to vote, and 381 of them say they intend to vote 'yes'.

What conclusions can you draw from this result?

Clearly your best estimate of the outcome of the referendum, based on this sample, is that 38.1% of the electorate will vote 'yes'. However, you know that a different sample would almost certainly have given a different result. You would be very surprised indeed if you took two random samples of 1000 and both contained 381 people who said that they intended voting 'yes'.

For your estimate of the outcome of the referendum to be useful, you really need some idea of the precision of your estimate. This is the case when you are making an estimate of any aspect of a population based on sample data, and it is the subject of this chapter.

Estimates and estimators

Before the referendum, there is some proportion of the parent population which intends voting 'yes'. This proportion is a *parameter* of the parent population. Assuming that voters do not change their minds (not always a valid assumption!), it is an actual, fixed number. You do not know the true value of this number until the referendum has taken place. The purpose of the opinion poll is to obtain an *estimate* of it, and in this case the obvious estimate is 0.381, which is the proportion of people in the sample who say that they intend voting 'yes'.

Prior to the referendum you cannot say whether your estimate is good or bad, since you do not have the true value of the *parameter* with which to compare it. In order to obtain some idea of how good or bad your estimate may be, you model it by a random variable. This random variable is called the *estimator* of the parameter. By looking at the properties of the estimator you can say something about the expected precision of your estimate. You can also decide how big a sample to use.

Setting up a model

You set up the model as follows.

- Let the number of people in the random sample of size one thousand who say that they intend voting 'yes' in the referendum be modelled by the random variable R.
- Let the true proportion of people in the population who intend voting 'yes' be p.

From *Statistics 1*, you know that R has a binomial distribution. In fact $R \sim B(1000, p)$. Once you have identified the model (binomial in this case) and specified the parameters of the model (sample size = 1000 and probability of 'success' = p) you may write down the probabilities of the various possible outcomes. Since the probability of success has not been given a numerical value, the probabilities will all be in terms of p. The general formula for these probabilities is

$$P(R = r) = \binom{1000}{r} p^r (1-p)^{1000-r} \text{ for } r= 0, 1, 2, \ldots, 1000.$$

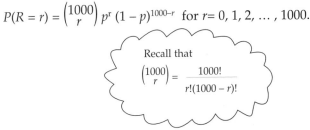

Recall that
$$\binom{1000}{r} = \frac{1000!}{r!(1000-r)!}$$

Here, r is called a realisation of the random variable R. Using r enables you to write a general formula for the probability of any possible outcome. By putting $r = 381$ and $p = 0.4$, you can work out the probability of exactly 381 people in a sample of 1000 saying they will vote 'yes', when the true proportion is 0.4.

From the model, you can also find the expected mean and variance. For the general binomial distribution, you know that the mean is np and the variance is $np(1-p)$. The following sections show how the modelling works in a variety of situations.

Simple random sample

Estimating a proportion

Suppose you wish to estimate the proportion of voters in a particular area who intend voting 'yes' in the referendum.

Suppose, also, that

- the parent population (the number of people in the area who are eligible to vote) is large and consists of N people
- the actual proportion of people who intend voting 'yes' is p
- a simple random sample of size n is selected
- each interviewee responds honestly
- each person in the sample knows whether or not s/he will vote 'yes'.

This ensures that there are only 2 options: there is no 'don't know' option

Your aim is to produce an estimate of p. It will be a number between zero and one, and you hope it will be near to the true value of p, the proportion of people in the area who intend voting 'yes'. The value of p is a fixed, but unknown, number: it is a parameter of the population. Your estimate would almost certainly be different if you chose a different random sample.

In the sample of prospective voters, you record the number of people who say that they intend voting 'yes'. The number of people in the sample who say that they intend voting 'yes' is modelled by the random variable R, and r is a realisation of R, i.e. the actual value obtained in a specific sample. The obvious estimator of p is the proportion in the sample who say that they would vote 'yes', so you model this by the random variable $\hat{P}$ and let a particular numerical value of the estimate be $\hat{p}$. (The use of a 'hat' to denote estimates and estimators is standard notation.)

Since r people in your sample of n people say that they intend to vote 'yes', the proportion of 'yes' voters in the sample is $\frac{r}{n}$. This is your estimate of p. You can write

$$\hat{p} = \frac{r}{n}$$

You model this by the random variable

$$\hat{P} = \frac{R}{n}.$$

Now, provided that the parent population is quite large, the random variable R has approximately a binomial distribution, so $R \sim B(n, p)$. You know (from *Statistics 2*) that the mean value of R is given by

$$E(R) = np$$

and that the variance of R is given by

$$Var(R) = npq$$

where $p + q = 1$.

You need to know how good an estimator $\hat{P}$ is for the true value of p. A good starting point is to calculate the expectation and variance of $\hat{P}$. The expectation of $\hat{P}$ is

$$E(\hat{P}) = E\left(\frac{R}{n}\right)$$

Recall that $E(kR) = kE(R)$

$$= \frac{E(R)}{n}$$

$$= \frac{np}{n}$$

$$= p.$$

The variance of $\hat{P}$ is given by

$$\text{Var}(\hat{P}) = \text{Var}(\tfrac{R}{n})$$

$$= \frac{\text{Var}(R)}{n^2}$$

Recall that $\text{Var}[kR] = k^2 \text{Var}[R]$

$$= \frac{npq}{n^2}$$

$$= \frac{pq}{n} \; .$$

Since the expected value of the estimator is equal to p, the parameter which it is being used to estimate, we say that $\hat{P}$ is an *unbiased estimator* of p. This means that if you take several samples and calculate estimates of p from each of these, the estimates will tend to centre on the correct value.

Since the variance of $\hat{P}$ tends to zero as n tends to infinity, we say that $\hat{P}$ is a *consistent estimator* of p. This means that estimates obtained from larger samples will tend to be closer to the true value than estimates obtained from smaller samples.

The conclusion of this is that if r people in a sample of size n said that they intended voting 'yes', then $\frac{r}{n}$ would be a sensible estimate of the proportion of 'yes' voters in the parent population.

This result should be reassuring rather than surprising. Indeed, it would have been very surprising if using $\frac{r}{n}$ had turned out not to be a good way of estimating the corresponding proportion in the whole population!

Finding a confidence interval for a proportion

An interviewer has just interviewed a simple random sample of 200 people and found that 82 said they intended voting 'no' in the referendum. Your best estimate of the proportion of people in the population who intend voting 'no' is therefore $\frac{82}{200}$, or 0.41.

One way of conveying something of the precision of this estimate is to give an interval rather than a single number. To do this, you need to know the variance of the estimator. In this case, the variance of $\hat{P}$ is $\frac{pq}{n}$. You cannot calculate this exactly because it is in terms of p, which you are trying to estimate.

What you can calculate from the sample data is an estimate of the variance of $\hat{P}$, namely

$$\frac{\hat{p}(1 - \hat{p})}{n}$$

A simple, and fairly standard, interval estimate of a parameter is found by going two estimated standard deviations above and below the point estimate.

Thus, the interval estimate for p is given by

$$\hat{p} \pm 2\sqrt{\frac{\hat{p}(1-\hat{p})}{n}}$$

For the opinion poll data, the estimated variance of the estimator is

$$\frac{0.41 \times 0.59}{200} = \frac{0.241\,9}{200} = 0.001\,209\,5.$$

The interval estimate is therefore

$0.41 \pm 2\sqrt{0.001\,209\,5} = 0.41 \pm 0.069\,5\ldots$ or $0.340\,4\ldots$ to $0.479\,5\ldots$.

So based on the results of the survey, a reasonable interval estimate of the percentage of the population who intend voting 'no' is from 34% to 48%.

If, instead, 820 people out of a sample of 2000 had said that they intended voting 'no', the point estimate would have remained unchanged at

$\frac{82}{200} = 0.41$ (or 41%). The interval estimate would change: it would now be

$$0.41 \pm 2\sqrt{\frac{0.41 \times 0.59}{2000}} = 0.41 \pm 0.0219\ldots \quad \text{or} \quad 0.3880\ldots \quad \text{to} \quad 0.4319\ldots$$

So based on a survey of ten times the number of people, the interval estimate would be much narrower: from 39% to 43%. As expected, a larger sample provides you with a narrower interval. Since the width of the interval depends on the standard deviation of $\hat{P}$ which has $\sqrt{n}$ in the denominator, you need to quadruple the sample size in order to halve the width of the interval.

This procedure for producing an interval estimate of the population proportion is almost equivalent in many situations to producing an approximate 95% confidence interval. Remember that the z values for a 95% confidence interval for the standard Normal distribution are ± 1.96. Using ± 2 standard deviations gives a slightly wider interval which serves as an approximate 95% confidence interval when the proportion is not too near zero or one.

NOTE

Using $\hat{p} \pm 2\sqrt{\frac{\hat{p}(1-\hat{p})}{n}}$ actually guarantees that you have at least a 75% confidence interval in any situation. This is due to a result by Tchebysheff which says that

$$P(|X - \mu| \geq k\sigma) \leq \frac{1}{k^2}.$$

When k=2 this gives $P(|X - \mu| \geq 2\sigma) \leq \frac{1}{4}$ which tells you that the probability that the random variable, X, is more than two standard deviations from the mean is less than 0.25. Consequently, the probability that X is within two standard deviations of the mean is more than 0.75.

The next example shows how you can use these ideas to help you decide what size of sample to take.

EXAMPLE

In a forthcoming US presidential election you know that the results are going to be close, with both main parties likely to poll around 35%, so you would like an interval estimate of the form $\pm 1\%$. Work out the sample size that you need in order to obtain the required precision.

Solution

Concentrating on one of the two parties, suppose that the proportion of people who intend voting for this party is p, and that the sample size is n.

The interval estimate for p will be $\hat{p} \pm 2\sqrt{\dfrac{\hat{p}(1-\hat{p})}{n}}$.

We need $2\sqrt{\dfrac{\hat{p}(1-\hat{p})}{n}}$ to be about 1%, which is 0.01.

Putting $\hat{p} = 0.35$ (using our knowledge of its approximate value) gives the equation

$$2\sqrt{\frac{0.35 \times 0.65}{n}} = 0.01.$$

Squaring each side gives $\quad 4 \times \dfrac{0.35 \times 0.65}{n} = 0.0001$.

So $n = 4 \times \dfrac{0.35 \times 0.65}{0.0001}$, which gives the sample size, n, as 9100.

This is a very large sample, larger than would normally be used. In practice, samples of between 1000 and 2000 are usually used.

In some situations, you would have no idea about the size of p. You still need to substitute some value in the formula $\hat{p} \pm 2\sqrt{\dfrac{\hat{p}(1-\hat{p})}{n}}$ in order to decide what sample size to use. In such cases you could use a pilot survey to provide a rough estimate. Alternatively you could use $p=0.5$. This gives a sample size which will always be large enough, since $p = 0.5$ is the case with the most variability.

The interval used for the estimate is $\hat{p} \pm 2\sqrt{\dfrac{\hat{p}(1-\hat{p})}{n}}$.

If you wish to find an interval estimate of the form $\hat{p} \pm \alpha$, so that the interval has width 2α, you need to solve the equation $2\sqrt{\dfrac{\hat{p}(1-\hat{p})}{n}} = \alpha.$

Squaring both sides gives $\quad 4\dfrac{\hat{p}(1-\hat{p})}{n} = \alpha^2,$

so $\dfrac{4\hat{p}(1-\hat{p})}{\alpha^2} = n.$

Analysis of surveys

23 | CIS

Commercial and industrial statistics

Thus $n = \dfrac{4\hat{p} - 4\hat{p}^2}{\alpha^2}$

$= \dfrac{1 - 1 + 4\hat{p} - 4\hat{p}^2}{\alpha^2}$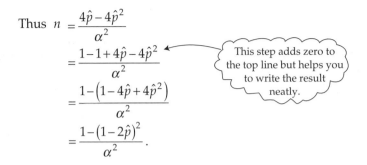

$= \dfrac{1 - \left(1 - 4\hat{p} + 4\hat{p}^2\right)}{\alpha^2}$

$= \dfrac{1 - \left(1 - 2\hat{p}\right)^2}{\alpha^2}.$

This step adds zero to the top line but helps you to write the result neatly.

Since you choose the value of α, the sample size depends only on the value of $\hat{p}$. The maximum value of the numerator is 1, and occurs when $\hat{p} = \frac{1}{2}$ (the expression in brackets is then equal to zero). Therefore, the maximum value of n is $\dfrac{1}{\alpha^2}$.

Estimating a total

If you wish to estimate the total number of voters (instead of the proportion of voters) who intend voting 'yes' in a referendum, you can use $N\hat{P}$ (where N is the size of the parent population) as the estimator, provided that N is known.

Suppose that the total number of voters in the referendum is 40 million, and your estimate of the proportion intending to vote 'yes' is 0.381, then your estimate of the total number of 'yes' votes is clearly

0.381×40 million $= 15.24$ million.

Exercise 2A

1. Jan owns a chain of video rental shops. She wants to estimate the proportion of customers who are dissatisfied with the videos they hire. If the proportion appears to be unacceptably high Jan intends investigating the matter further. Initially she chooses a simple random sample of 500 customers from one day. The shop assistants ask the customers to fill in a one-question questionnaire when they return their videos. While she is awaiting the responses, Jan realises that she has no idea of the precision of the estimate that she will obtain. Provide a conservative estimate for her.

2. The owner of a daily newspaper wishes to estimate the proportion of its readers who are against a possible merger with another daily paper. It is thought that about 75% of the readers are against the merger, and the estimate is required to be within 5% of the true value. How large a simple random sample should be used?

3. You are planning a survey of voting intentions in the lead-up to a referendum, and you have no idea what proportion of the electors intend to vote 'yes'. You would like your estimate of the proportion to have a precision of ±5%. Use $p = 0.5$ to find the size of sample that is required.

4. Readers of a popular newspaper have been complaining since a change in ownership that too many grammatical and spelling errors are appearing in it. The publishers believe that fewer than 10% of

CIS | 24

pages contain more than one such error. In order to assess the actual magnitude of the problem, they have decided to check a random sample of pages from the papers printed since the change in ownership. To estimate to within 1% the number of pages with at least one error, how large a sample is needed?

5. Most opinion polls for national elections use a sample size of about 2000. By using $p = 0.5$, give a pessimistic value of the precision this gives in estimating the proportion of voters who intend voting for a particular party.

6. A local council is considering offering grants to council house tenants to bring their loft insulation up to the recommended thickness. It needs to estimate the number of houses that would qualify for the grant. In a random sample of size 50, there are 7 houses that would qualify for the grant.

(i) Produce an approximate 95% confidence interval for the proportion of houses which would qualify for the grant, based on this sample.

(ii) There are actually 20 000 council houses in the area. Calculate an approximate 95% confidence interval for the number of houses that would qualify for a grant.

7. A publisher is considering starting a new magazine for physiotherapists. The potential market is about 50 000 people and he wishes to know whether the magazine would be viable. He decides to pay a market research organisation to carry out a survey for him. He estimates that about half of the people might buy the paper if he keeps the price low enough. If he is willing to accept an estimate with a precision of ± 500, how large a sample should the organisation use?

Estimating the mean from numerical responses

The editor of a popular music magazine wants to estimate the average amount of money which the readers of the magazine spend on music CDs each month. This situation differs from the earlier examples in this chapter because here the responses are numerical (an amount of money) rather than categorical. The editor includes a questionnaire in one issue of the magazine, and 200 readers returned it correctly completed.

The amount of money, $£x_i$, that each respondent claims to spend on CDs per month is recorded. The data are summarised as

$$\sum_{i=1}^{200} x_i = 2149 \quad \text{and} \quad \sum_{i=1}^{200} x_i^2 = 23\,853.$$

The obvious estimate for the mean amount of money spent per month on music CDs by all readers is

$$£\bar{x} = £\frac{2149}{200} = £10.745.$$

However, you need to know something about the precision of this estimate, so you need to model the situation.

In order to do this you need to make some assumptions. The first is that the readers who return the questionnaire are a representative sample. The second is that the parent population is large and the sample is a relatively small proportion of it. If these assumptions are valid then you may adequately model the amounts of money $x_1, x_2, ..., x_n$ by the independent random variables $X_1, X_2, ..., X_n$,

where $E[X_i] = \mu$ and $Var[X_i] = \sigma^2$ for $i = 1, ..., n$.

In other words, you assume that the random variables are independent (because you chose a random sample) and that they all have the same distribution, with mean μ and variance σ^2.

You now wish to use $\bar{x}$ as an estimate for μ, and to say something about the precision of this estimate. As usual, you need to consider the corresponding random variable, $\bar{X}$, in order to be able to make comments about precision.

You know from *Statistics 3* that

$$E[\bar{X}] = \mu \quad \text{and} \quad Var[\bar{X}] = \frac{\sigma^2}{n}.$$

This tells you that $\bar{X}$ is an unbiased and a consistent estimator for μ.

As you do not know the value of σ^2, you need to estimate it from the sample data. The unbiased estimator of σ^2 is

$$\hat{\sigma}^2 = \frac{\sum_{i=1}^{n}(x_i - \bar{x})^2}{n-1} .$$

However, if n is large it makes little difference whether you use n or $(n-1)$ in the denominator. Just as when you were estimating proportions, you can find an approximate 95% confidence interval using $\bar{x} \pm 2\dfrac{\hat{\sigma}}{\sqrt{n}}$.

In the music magazine example, you have $\bar{x} = \dfrac{\sum x_i}{200} = \dfrac{2149}{200} = 10.745$.

The variance of the data is

$$s^2 = \frac{\sum(x_i - \bar{x})^2}{200} = \frac{\sum x_1^2}{200} - \bar{x}^2 = \frac{23\,853}{200} - 10.745^2 = 3.80...$$

The estimate of the mean amount spent per month on CDs by the readers of the magazine is £10.745. The level of precision implied by giving all five figures is misleading: it would be more appropriate to quote the answer as £10.70 (to the nearest 10p), £10.50 (to the nearest 50p) or £11 (to the nearest pound). It might be more useful, though, to express the estimate as an approximate 95% confidence interval. In order to do this, you need an estimate of the standard deviation of the population from which the sample was taken. The simplest estimate to use is the standard deviation of the sample data:

$$s = \sqrt{3.80} ... = 1.951 ...$$

Using this, the approximate 95% confidence interval is

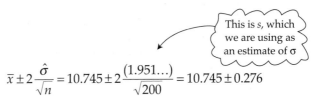

This is s, which we are using as an estimate of σ

$$\bar{x} \pm 2\frac{\hat{\sigma}}{\sqrt{n}} = 10.745 \pm 2\frac{(1.951...)}{\sqrt{200}} = 10.745 \pm 0.276$$

This is [10.468... , 11.021...], which is [10.47, 11.02] to the nearest penny.

A sensible way of expressing this result is to say that most readers of the magazine spend between £10.50 and £11.00 on music CDs per month.

NOTE

If you use the unbiased estimator $\hat{\sigma}^2 = \dfrac{\sum(x_2 - \bar{x})^2}{n-1}$ *you obtain* $\hat{\sigma} = 1.956$ *...This*

gives the same confidence interval, correct to the nearest penny.

Estimating the total from numerical responses

The music magazine editor might well wish to estimate the total amount of money spent per month by its readers. If the number of copies of the magazine sold in the month of the survey was 23 652, what would be your estimate of the total expenditure of the readers on CDs per month, expressed both as a single number (a point estimate) and as an interval?

As you would expect, the point and interval estimates of the total are obtained simply by multiplying the point and interval estimates of the mean by the size of the parent population (see question **1** in exercise 2B).

Exercise 2B

1. A simple random sample $x_1, x_2, ..., x_n$ from a parent population of size N is modelled by the independent random variables $X_1, X_2, ..., X_n$ where $E(X_i) = \mu$ and $Var(X_i) = \sigma^2$ for $i = 1, ...,n$.
The total is estimated using $N\bar{x}$, which we model by $N\bar{X}$.
   (i) Show that $N\bar{X}$ is unbiased and consistent as an estimator of the total $(N\mu)$.
   (ii) Calculate the point and approximate 95% confidence interval estimates for the amount of money spent per month by the readers of the magazine, using the data given in the text above.

2. An insurance company is to launch a new house contents policy. It will not require the householder to estimate the value of each item of property in order to decide upon the amount of cover they should have. Instead, the company is to set some standard amount of cover, which should be sufficient for most householders. In order to estimate what this level of cover should be, the company chooses random samples of households in three different areas A, B and C. An employee of the company visits each household (once permission has been obtained), to estimate the value of the house contents. Initially, the company treats each area separately.

Area	$\sum_{i=1}^{50} x_i$ (thousands)	$\sum_{i=1}^{50} x_i^2$ (millions)	Sample size
A	254	1 435	50
B	759	11 979	50
C	1 489	46 006	50

(i) Use the data to estimate (a) the average value of the contents in households in each of the areas, and (b) the standard deviation of the value of the contents for each area.

(ii) To decide on a figure that is sufficient to cover most of the households, the company uses $\bar{x} + 3\hat{\sigma}$. If the values of the household contents in each area are reasonably Normally distributed, what proportion of households will find the level of insurance cover insufficient?

(iii) From the results of the survey, what level of cover should be adequate for most households in area A?

(iv) What are the corresponding values for areas B and C?

(v) Do you think that the company's initial idea of one single policy is a good one in the light of the data obtained from the survey? If not, could you suggest an alternative idea?

3. A grower of soft fruit wonders whether it is better to pay workers to harvest the fruit for her or to allow people to pick the fruit themselves. If she were to pay workers to pick the fruit she would expect the yield to be higher. In order to investigate this she decides to take a random sample of 10 blackcurrant bushes, mark them so that the public do not pick their fruit, and pick and weigh the fruit herself. She has a total of 286 bushes so she wants to estimate the total yield, and hence the income, which she could obtain by paying workers to pick all of the fruit.

The weights of the blackcurrants she picked from the 10 bushes are given below (in kg).

5.29 5.25 4.40 4.28 4.81 5.07 4.78
5.54 4.69 4.07

Find an approximate 95% confidence interval for the total weight of fruit which she would have obtained from her 286 bushes.

Systematic sample

If the parent population is in no particular order in terms of the item of interest, we use the same formulae as for a simple random sample to calculate point and interval estimates of the population mean, total or proportion.

However, if it is in order corresponding to the item of interest, the large values are known to occur together, as are the smaller values, and so there is some correlation between successive values. They are not independent as they would be in a simple random sample. In this case, we may still use the same formulae for point estimates of the mean or the total, but the variance estimate will tend to be too large and so the interval will also tend to be too large.

Stratified sample

A local radio station wishes to estimate the proportion of people in the main city in the region who listen to it and the amount of time which people spend listening to radio generally. To investigate these questions it takes a sample stratified by age, with stratum sizes proportional to the number of people in each age group at the most recent census. The people were asked if they had listened to the local station in the previous week and how many hours of (any) radio they had listen to in the previous week. The results are given in the table below.

Age group	Population at last census to the nearest thousand	Number in sample	Number listening to local station	Proportion of age group listening to local station	Average number of hours per week spent listening to radio
	N	n	r	$\hat{p} = \frac{r}{n}$	$\bar{x}$
15 to 19	14 000	56	45	0.804	15.3
20 to 24	26 000	104	73	0.702	12.8
25 to 34	60 000	240	58	0.242	6.7
35 to 44	52 000	208	41	0.197	8.1
45 to 54	31 000	124	35	0.282	9.4
55 to 64	39 000	156	86	0.551	11.6
65 and over	49 000	196	149	0.760	18.5

The best estimate of the total number of people in the city who listen to the local radio station at some time in a week is

$$\Sigma N\hat{p} = 14\,000 \times 0.804 + 26\,000 \times 0.702 + 60\,000 \times 0.242 + 52\,000 \times 0.197 +$$
$$31\,000 \times 0.282 + 39\,000 \times 0.551 + 49\,000 \times 0.760$$

$$= 121\,743$$

The best estimate of the proportion of people who listen to the local radio station at some time in the week is

$$\frac{\Sigma N\hat{p}}{\Sigma N} = \frac{121\,743}{271\,000} \quad \text{which is 0.449 or about 45\%.}$$

The best estimate of the total amount of time people in the city spend listening to the radio in a week is

$$\Sigma N\bar{x} = 14\,000 \times 15.3 + 26\,000 \times 12.8 + 60\,000 \times 6.7 + 52\,000 \times 8.1 +$$
$$31\,000 \times 9.4 + 39\,000 \times 11.6 + 49\,000 \times 18.5$$

$$= 3\,020\,500.$$

The best estimate of the average amount of time per week which people in the city spend listening to the radio is

$$\frac{\Sigma N\bar{x}}{\Sigma N} = \frac{3\,020\,500}{271\,000} \quad \text{which is 11.146 hours or just over 11 hours.}$$

In the case of stratified sampling, the use of the sample variances to estimate the precision of the results is more complicated than for simple random sampling, so we shall not deal with it in this book.

Cluster sample

The formulae used to obtain point estimates from a cluster sample are the same as the ones used for stratified samples. Again, the estimation of variances is complicated and so you shall not deal with it in this book.

Exercise 2C

1. Panorama PC, a computer retailer, wishes to estimate the proportion of homes in its vicinity which possess a computer. For those that have a computer, Panorama would also like to know how long it is since the computer was bought or upgraded. This information is to be used to plan a marketing campaign. Panorama's market researcher decides to use a telephone survey with a sample size of 2000. As the sampling frame, she uses the telephone directory for the area, which contains 300 000 entries. She uses systematic sampling.

In the sample of 2000 homes, 379 have one or more computers.

For those homes with a computer, the information about the time x (in years) since the computer was bought or upgraded is summarised as follows:

$\Sigma x = 1185.81$ and $\Sigma x^2 = 4554.756$.

Use these data to calculate point estimates and approximate 95% confidence intervals for the proportion of homes in this area which have a computer and for the length of time since the computer was bought/upgraded.

2. In a hospital, detailed patient records are kept in files. There is also a database containing the summary details of each of the 60 000 patients. The database is organised in order of patient number,

which does not impose any structure on the records.

A tracer card has been printed out for each patient; this contains the summary information that is stored on the database. The tracer cards are stored with the detailed patient records, and are used as place-holders when the detailed records are removed.

The records administrator is concerned that the tracer cards are becoming tattered, so that many need replacing. In order to decide whether extra staff will be needed to produce the new cards, the administrator needs an estimate of the number to be replaced, with a precision of ± 1000 (since she thinks that 1000 cards will take about 1 person day to produce). What sample size should she use?

3. The table gives suitable notation for a stratified sample with 3 strata.

Stratum	Stratum size	Stratum proportion	Sample size	Number in sample with characteristic	Sample proportion
A	N_a	p_a	n_a	r_a	$\hat{p}_a$
B	N_b	p_b	n_b	r_b	$\hat{p}_b$
C	N_c	p_c	n_c	r_c	$\hat{p}_c$

Show that the estimators corresponding to $N_a\hat{p}_a + N_b\hat{p}_b + N_c\hat{p}_c$ and to

Exercise 2C continued

$$\frac{N_a\hat{p}_a + N_b\hat{p}_b + N_c\hat{p}_c}{N_a + N_b + N_c}$$

are unbiased and consistent for the population total and the population proportion respectively.

4. An insurance company suspects that many of its clients have insufficient insurance for the value of their house contents. The company also believes that those people with the larger cover will tend to be under-insured to a larger extent than those who are insured for smaller amounts. Someone with only £10 000 of contents insurance may be under-insured by about £1000, but someone with £30 000 cover may well be under-insured by about £5000. In order to investigate this, they decide to send a representative to visit a sample of 200 customers.

   (i) Explain why it would be advantageous to use a systematic sample from the database of clients after sorting it according to the amount for which the clients have insured their goods.

   (ii) The results of the survey on the level of under-insurance were $\Sigma x = 721\ 950$ and $\Sigma x^2 = 3\ 430\ 200\ 000$ for the sample of 200 customers. Calculate a conservative 95% confidence interval for the mean level of under-insurance.

   (iii) Can you suggest a better way to look at the data?

5. The editor of a regional newspaper monitors the size of the readership in a number of different ways. One way is the number of copies which are sold. However, it is well known that many copies are read by more than one person. Therefore a regular survey is also conducted when interviewees are asked whether they read the paper yesterday (giving the issue readership) and whether they read it in the preceding seven days (giving the weekly readership). The results of one such survey are shown in the table below. Estimate the total issue readership and the total weekly readership of the newspaper.

Age	Population at last census (thousands)	Average issue readership (%)	Average weekly readership (%)
15 to 19	14	8	12
20 to 24	26	13	19
25 to 34	60	28	43
35 to 44	52	28	38
45 to 54	31	21	24
55 to 64	39	21	27
65 +	49	28	31

6. In a survey to estimate the total area (in acres) used for growing corn all of the farms in a region were first stratified according to size. The number of farms in each stratum is shown in the table below.

Stratum	1	2	3	4	5	6	7	Total
Number	394	461	391	334	169	113	148	2010

   (i) Consideration of costs limits the sample size to about one hundred. Using proportional allocation determine the appropriate sample sizes for each stratum.

   (ii) The means and the standard deviations obtained for each stratum are given in the table below. Estimate the total area (in acres) used for growing corn.

Stratum	1	2	3	4	5	6	7
Mean	5.4	16.3	24.3	34.5	42.1	50.1	63.8
Standard deviation	8.3	13.3	15.1	19.8	24.5	26.0	35.2

Exercise 2C continued

(iii) Within what limits do you think the true value lies? (Just make a guess, do not try to do any calculations.)

7. In a survey to find out the area in hectares used for growing oilseed rape, farms were stratified according to the area that they had said was used for oilseed rape in an earlier census. The numbers in the sample from each stratum were intended to be 7% of the stratum total, giving proportional allocation. However, due to some farmers not returning their questionnaires the numbers in the stratum samples were not quite what would have been required for proportional allocation. A summary of the results from the survey is given in the table below.

Stratum	1	2	3	Total
Σx (ha)	3075	5680	10162	–
Σx^2 (ha^2)	30848	122440	538638	–
Stratum size	5472	4231	3853	13556
Sample size	353	276	218	847

(i) Use these results to estimate the total area given to growing oilseed rape.
(ii) What percentage of farms did not respond to the questionnaire? How much might this affect your estimate?
(iii) Within what limits do you think the total area should lie? (Just guess, do not do any calculations.)

Unknown population or strata sizes

For most of this chapter, it has been assumed that an adequate sampling frame could be produced for the parent population. Sometimes it is possible to make progress even without a sampling frame.

For example, in a telephone survey covering one dialling-code area, the first part of the number – the area code – may be kept fixed and then the final part of the number may be chosen using the random number generator on a computer. This should result in a satisfactory random sample, but the size of the parent population may not be known. From the sample data it would be possible to produce estimates of population proportions and means, using the formulae given earlier. It would not be possible to produce estimates of totals, because the size of the parent population is required for this.

If you wish to use stratified sampling to estimate the proportion of a population which has a specific characteristic, you actually need to know only the relative sizes of the strata, and not their actual sizes. The same is true if you wish to estimate the average value of some feature of the population. In some cases it may be relatively easy to determine the stratum to which an element of the population belongs, but it may be harder to obtain the information in which you are really interested. In this situation you could use what is called *double sampling* to obtain your estimate.

For example, a large baking firm wants to improve its impact on a particular city. The marketing manager plans to use a detailed questionnaire to find out about the amount and types of bread, cakes, etc. that households eat. The households in the area are to be stratified by age and type – young, middle aged or pensioners, single occupiers, couples, families, etc. Since the stratum sizes are not known, the method of double sampling is used.

First a large random sample is taken, and each household is put into the appropriate stratum. This enables the relative sizes of the strata to be estimated. The second stage is to use the list of households that have been allocated to the strata, and to select a sample from each stratum proportional to the estimated size of the stratum. These households are then asked to answer the detailed questionnaire. Since the relative sizes of the strata have been estimated, the results of the detailed questionnaire may be used to estimate proportions and means, using the usual formulae for stratified samples. Since the actual sizes of the strata are not known, the results may not be used to estimate totals. The formulae for estimating the variance are complex because of the special nature of the situation and so we shall not deal with them in this book.

Post-stratification

A market research organisation is investigating the average amount of time spent on fitness activities by people in a particular area, who are not in full-time education. The survey has been commissioned by a company planning to open a fitness centre in the area. It seems reasonable that the survey should be stratified according to age and to sex. It is to be done using telephone interviews. However, the age and sex of the person answering the telephone will not be known until they answer the phone, so the sample cannot be chosen in advance from the relevant strata. Instead, respondents will be put into the correct strata after they have been interviewed. This is called post-stratification.

Using post-stratification, the formulae for the estimates of proportions, means and totals are just the same as for pre-stratification. The variance estimates are more complex, and we shall not deal with them in this book.

Estimating the size of the population: capture-recapture

The manager of a fish farm wishes to estimate the number of trout which he has in one tank. He captures and marks 25 fish from the tank, then releases them and allows them to circulate again. He then takes another sample of size 50. He finds that 7 of these are marked.

The proportion of fish in the second sample that are marked is $\frac{7}{50}$. The manager can take this as an estimate of the proportion of fish in the whole section that are marked. Since he knows that the total number of marked fish is 25, he can write

$$\frac{25}{N} \approx \frac{7}{50}$$

where N is the total number in the tank.

So his estimate of N is given by

$$\hat{N} = \frac{25 \times 50}{7}$$

$$= 178.57\ldots$$

He concludes that there are about 180 trout in the tank.

This method of estimating the size of a population is often used in zoology, and is called *capture–recapture*. It is a reliable method provided that the population is contained within a closed area, such as a tank, an island or a game reserve (so that immigration and emigration are not major factors) and provided that the animals mix freely within the closed area.

To express the mathematics of the method in general terms you need to define some notation. Let

N be the total population,
m be the number of animals captured and marked,
s be the total number of animals in the recaptured sample,
t be the number of marked animals in the recaptured sample.

Then

$$\frac{t}{s} \approx \frac{m}{N} \quad \text{or} \quad N \approx \frac{ms}{t}$$

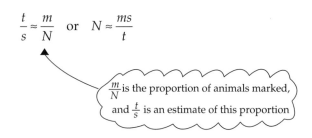

$\frac{m}{N}$ is the proportion of animals marked, and $\frac{t}{s}$ is an estimate of this proportion

Activity

1. A trade union organising a protest rally in London wishes to estimate the number of people who are present at the rally. As the protesters gather at a large central location, 500 of them are given bright yellow cards. The cards are given out in as random a manner as possible. If there is an obvious group of protesters, only one of them is given a card. Between two of the speeches in the rally, a section of the crowd is clearly identified, and the people in that section having yellow cards are asked to hold them up. The total number of people in the section is found to be 240 and the number holding cards is 14.
   (i) What is your estimate of the total number of people at the rally?
   (ii) Do you think this is a good method of estimation in this situation? Write down any weaknesses that you can identify.
2. Investigate capture–recapture using simulation, either by hand or using a computer.
   (i) With a population of 10 000, how many individuals must you catch and mark if you wish to estimate the population to the nearest 1000?
   (ii) What happens to the precision of your estimate if you double the number of individuals that you catch and mark?

Embarrassing questions

There are occasions when interviewees may not be willing to answer a question, or when they may deliberately give a false answer. For example, if the question is about tax matters, interviewees may be concerned that an honest response may lead to their being prosecuted! If a medical researcher is studying drug abuse by school pupils, interviewees may again be tempted to give false responses because they are afraid of their parents or the law, even if the interviewer tries to assure them that their individual responses will not be communicated to anyone else.

There are two standard ways of overcoming this problem. Both involve the interviewee using some random method to choose between two questions, so that the interviewer does not know which of the two questions the interviewee is answering. Probability theory is then used to estimate the proportion of people who answered 'yes' to the question of interest.

For example, suppose that a director of a company wishes to find out about the attitudes of employees to a particular manager. She wishes to ask a random sample of employees the question

> *Do you think that the manager should be fired?*

Employees might well be concerned that a positive response would find its way back to the manager and that they would be in trouble.

Cards method

This method involves using a pack of cards, in which a known proportion are marked 'A' and the rest 'B'. The interviewee is presented with two opposite versions (A and B) of the same question, and answers the version corresponding to the card drawn at random from the pack.

In this example the two versions of the question would be

> A: *Do you think that the manager should be fired?*

> B: *Do you think that the manager should stay?*

An employee who thinks that the manager should be fired will answer 'yes' to question A and 'no' to question B. An employee who thinks that the manager should stay will answer 'no' to question A and 'yes ' to question B. The interviewer does not know which question the employee is answering, so the employee should feel secure and able to answer the question honestly.

How do you analyse the results? Suppose that $\frac{2}{3}$ of the cards are labelled 'A' and that out of a sample of 100, 60 employees answer 'yes' and 40 answer 'no'. If the actual proportion of employees who believe that the manager should be fired is p, the situation may be represented as in the tree diagram in figure 2.1.

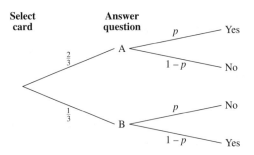

Figure 2.1

The probability of a 'yes' response is given by

$$\frac{2}{3}p + \frac{1}{3}(1-p) = \frac{2p+1-p}{3} = \frac{p+1}{3}.$$

This should be approximately equal to the proportion of 'yes' responses obtained, which was $\frac{60}{100}$. So you can write

$$\frac{p+1}{3} \approx \frac{60}{100}$$

This gives

$$p \approx \frac{3 \times 60}{100} - 1 \quad \Rightarrow \quad p \approx 0.8 .$$

From these data, it appears that about 80% of the employees think that the manager should be fired.

If the vast majority of the cards in the pack were labelled 'A', the interviewees would feel less confident about answering the questions because the interviewer would be fairly sure that they were answering question 'A'. This would defeat the purpose of the method. However, if exactly half of the cards were labelled 'A' it would not be possible to use the results of the interviews to estimate the proportion in which you are interested. You can see why by working through the next activity.

Activity

Draw a tree diagram for the general situation in which the proportion of cards marked 'A' is θ, and the proportion marked 'B' is $1 - \theta$.
(i) Write an expression in terms of p and θ for the probability of a 'yes' response.
(ii) Put your answer to (i) equal to $\frac{y}{n}$, where y is the number of 'yes' responses and n is the total number of interviewees. Make p the subject of the formula to obtain an estimate for p.
(iii) What happens to the expression in (i) and to your estimate for p when when $\theta = \frac{1}{2}$?

You should have found the estimate of p to be $\dfrac{\frac{y}{n} - (1-\theta)}{2\theta - 1}$, so your estimator

of p is $\hat{P} = \dfrac{\frac{Y}{n} - (1-\theta)}{2\theta - 1}$.

To find out something about the precision of your estimate, or to decide the sample size required to give a particular degree of precision, you need to consider the variance of your estimator. The number of 'yes' responses, y, is the sum of those who answered 'yes' to question A and those who answered 'yes' to question B. So provided that the parent population is large compared with the size of the sample, you can write

$$Y \sim B[n, (2\theta - 1)p + (1 - \theta)]$$

So $E(Y) = n[(2\theta - 1)p + (1 - \theta)]$

and $Var(Y) = n[(2\theta - 1)p + (1 - \theta)][1 - (2\theta - 1)p - (1 - \theta)]$

$$= n[(2\theta - 1)p + (1 - \theta)][\theta - (2\theta - 1)p].$$

Hence $E(\hat{P}) = E\left[\dfrac{\frac{Y}{n} - (1-\theta)}{2\theta - 1}\right]$

$$= \dfrac{\frac{1}{n}E[Y] - (1-\theta)}{2\theta - 1}.$$

$\theta \neq \frac{1}{2}$ so that the denominator $\neq 0$

Substituting for $E[Y]$ and simplifying gives $E[\hat{P}] = p$.

This shows that $\hat{P}$ is an unbiased estimator for p.

The variance of $\hat{P}$ is

$$Var(\hat{P}) = Var\left[\dfrac{\frac{Y}{n} - (1-\theta)}{2\theta - 1}\right]$$

$$= \dfrac{\frac{1}{n^2}Var[Y]}{(2\theta - 1)^2}$$

Again $\theta \neq \frac{1}{2}$

$$= \dfrac{n[(2\theta - 1)p + (1 - \theta)][\theta - (2\theta - 1)p]}{n^2(2\theta - 1)^2}$$

$$= \dfrac{[(2\theta - 1)p + (1 - \theta)][\theta - (2\theta - 1)p]}{n(2\theta - 1)^2}$$

Since this expression tends to zero as n tends to infinity, $\hat{P}$ is a consistent estimator for p. The expression could also be used to provide the confidence interval form of an estimate of p, or to find an appropriate sample size for a specified precision, provided that an approximate value of p could be supplied.

CIS

Activity

In the situation described on p35, in which 100 people were asked whether a manager should be sacked, $\frac{2}{3}$ of the cards were labelled 'A' and 60 people responded 'yes'. The resulting estimate of p was 0.8.

(i) Check that the general formula given above for estimating p gives the same value for p.

(ii) Use the estimated value of p in the formula for the variance of $\hat{P}$ to estimate the variance in this case.

(iii) Show that the approximate 95% confidence interval for the proportion is

$$\frac{4}{5} \pm 2 \times \frac{3}{50} \quad \text{or} \quad (0.68, 0.92).$$

(iv) What can you conclude from these results?

Coin-tossing method

A second method for persuading interviewees to answer embarrassing questions honestly involves tossing a coin twice. Again there are two questions, but this time one of them is completely irrelevant to the issue. Which question is answered depends on the outcome of the first toss of the coin.

The director with management problems might decide to use this method, asking each employee to spin a coin twice. The two questions are

A: *Do you think that the manager should be fired?*
B: *Did you get heads on the second throw of the coin?*

Interviewees who obtain 'heads' on the first throw answer question 'A', the others answer question 'B'. For each interviewee, the probability of answering question A is $\frac{1}{2}$. For those who answer question B, the probability of a 'yes' response is also $\frac{1}{2}$.

Let the actual proportion of employees who think that the manager should be fired be p. The situation is represented in figure 2.2.

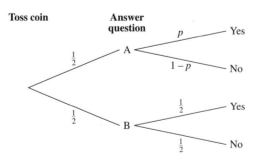

Figure 2.2

In a sample of 200 employees taking part in this survey, the director receives 130 'yes' responses. What does this tell you?

Roughly half of the sample would get 'tails' on their first spin of the coin and would therefore answer question 'B', and roughly half of these would obtain 'heads' on their second spin of the coin and would therefore answer 'yes'. So, about 50 of the 'yes' responses are accounted for. That leaves about 80 which are probably due to interviewees answering the 'real' question about the manager. Since about 100 of them were probably answering this question, it appears that the proportion of employees who think that the manager should be fired is about $\frac{80}{100}$, or 80%.

In order to answer questions about the precision of your estimate, you need to formalise this argument using the tree diagram and the normal rules of probability, as was done for the 'cards' method. The following activity guides you through this.

Activity

(i)   Use the tree diagram to obtain a general expression (in terms of p) for the probability of a 'yes' response using this method.
(ii)   Write the proportion of yes responses obtained in the example above.
(iii)   Using your answers to (i) and (ii), show that the resulting estimate for p is again $p \approx 0.8$.

Now suppose that there were y 'yes' responses from n interviewees.

(iv)   Put $\frac{y}{n}$ equal to your answer for part (i) and rearrange it to obtain an estimate for p.
(v)   Show that the estimator of p is

$$\hat{P} = \frac{2Y}{n} - 0.5$$

where Y is the random variable modelling the number of 'yes' responses.

As before, provided that the number of employees is large, Y has approximately a binomial distribution. In this case

$$Y \sim B(n, 0.5p + 0.25).$$

The expected value of Y is

$$E(Y) = n[0.5p + 0.25].$$

The variance of Y is

$$\text{Var}(Y) = n[0.5p + 0.25][0.75 - 0.5p].$$

Using these, you can find the expected value of the estimator, $\hat{P}$:

$$E(\hat{P}) = E\left[\frac{2Y}{n} - 0.5\right]$$
$$= \frac{2E(Y)}{n} - 0.5$$
$$= p.$$

Analysis of surveys

39 CIS

2

The variance of $\hat{P}$ is

$$
\begin{aligned}
\mathrm{Var}\left[\hat{P}\right] &= \mathrm{Var}\left[\frac{2Y}{n}\right] - 0.5 \\
&= \frac{4\,\mathrm{Var}(Y)}{n^2} \\
&= \frac{4n[0.5p + 0.25][0.75 - 0.5p]}{n^2} \\
&= \frac{[2p + 1][3 - 2p]}{4n}.
\end{aligned}
$$

This shows you that this estimator, too, is unbiased and consistent for p. Having found a formula for the variance you may, as usual, use this to estimate the precision of an estimate or to decide upon a sample size provided that you have an initial estimate of the value of p.

By rewriting $\mathrm{Var}[\hat{P}]$ in the form

$$
\mathrm{Var}\left(\hat{P}\right) = \frac{4 - (2p - 1)^2}{4n}
$$

you can see that the largest variance occurs when $p = \frac{1}{2}$, since the term in brackets is then zero. The variance in this case is $\frac{1}{n}$. If you do not have an initial estimate for p, you can use $\frac{1}{n}$ as a worst case value for the variance.

Excercise 2D

1. In a national firm, a director wishes to find out the opinion of the workers in a particular area about the area manager. A sample of 800 people are interviewed and 340 respond 'yes'. If there are 20 cards labelled 'A' and 30 cards labelled 'B', estimate the proportion of employees who think that the manager should be fired. What is the approximate 95% confidence interval for this proportion?

2. Calculate the variance of the estimate of p for $p = 0.1, 0.2, 0.3, ..., 0.9$ and for $\theta = 0.1, 0.2$, 0.3 and 0.4 when 500 people are interviewed. Present the results in a table.

Value of θ	Value of p								
	0.1	0.2	0.3	0.4	0.5	0.6	0.7	0.8	0.9
0.1									
0.2									
0.3									
0.4									

3. You are a market researcher. You have been asked by the police to interview a random sample of young people about whether they have ever used illegal drugs of any kind. You decide to use the method of tossing a coin twice.
   (i) Write down what you will say to each interviewee to convince them that their answers cannot possibly identify them as drug users. (Remember that it is important to standardise procedures like this, so it is often necessary to work from a script.)
   You interview 100 young people and you obtain 34 'yes' responses.
   (ii) Estimate the proportion of young people who have used illegal drugs. What is the approximate 95% confidence interval for this proportion?
   (iii) Suppose instead that you had interviewed 1000 young people and obtained 340 'yes' responses. Estimate the proportion of young people who have used illegal drugs in this case.

What would be the approximate 95% confidence interval for this proportion?

4. A large company wishes to find out whether its female employees are being sexually harassed. It uses the cards method. A box of 15 cards is provided; 9 marked 'A' and 6 marked 'B'. If the woman being interviewed chooses a card marked 'A', she is asked to respond 'yes' or 'no' to the statement

'I have been the subject of sexual harassment during the last 12 months.'

If the woman chooses a card marked 'B', she is asked to respond 'yes' or 'no' to the statement,

'I have been free of sexual harassment for the last 12 months.'

There are 221 'yes' responses and 279 'no' responses. Estimate the proportion of women who have been sexually harassed in the last 12 months, and give a 95% confidence interval for this proportion.

Finding other information from surveys

In this chapter you have looked at ways of selecting a sample in order to estimate a proportion, a mean, a total or the population size. In practice, the aim of the survey may be to find an estimate of a single population parameter or indeed of several parameters. This could be achieved using the methods you have met in this chapter.

Sometimes you may be interested in interactions between several factors. You may be looking for correlations rather than for means and proportions. For example, you might conduct a questionnaire about diet, exercise and health in order to find correlations between skin problems and diet, between heart disease and exercise and so on.

In these cases, the method of selecting the sample would follow the principles you have met in this chapter, but the analysis would proceed along different lines. For bivariate continuous data, regression or correlation techniques would probably be useful. For categorical data, contingency tables and χ^2 tests might be appropriate.

If the data have been collected in a reasonable way then it is worth taking the time to analyse them sensibly. You should always draw stemplots and boxplots of small data sets, and histograms and cumulative frequency plots of larger data sets. A plot tells you much more than just an average. If the data appear to be approximately Normally distributed, it is probably worth checking this with a probability plot.

One danger in analysing data is to be too short-sighted. It is often helpful to step back from the data and look at it in a broader context. It is also helpful to look up previous research to find out what is already known on an issue: you will rarely find yourself conducting a survey on an issue that has not been studied elsewhere. Looking at other studies often helps you to avoid pitfalls. It may sometimes suggest what kind of answer you will obtain, and in some cases it might even make your survey unnecessary.

Meta-analysis

Surveys are usually very time-consuming and expensive to conduct. It is often much more economical to use results that other studies have generated, rather than to start again from scratch. Sometimes, by looking at several surveys which individually produced inconclusive results, useful conclusions can be drawn. For example, several national surveys might have been done on the link between diet and health, without showing any significant link. However, if the results of these surveys were combined, they might well lead to some significant conclusions. This is the basic principle of *meta-analysis*.

Sometimes survey results are from different areas and sometimes they may be from different years. It is not always valid simply to combine results in the obvious way: the techniques of meta-analysis are required in order to avoid drawing false conclusions. Meta-analysis is a relatively new subject area, although its roots go back at least as far as Karl Pearson in 1904. The methodology has developed considerably in the last two decades, partly because of the increased computing power available. The detail of meta-analysis is beyond the scope of this book, but it is important to be aware of its existence.

KEY POINTS

After working through this chapter you should
- understand the difference between an estimate and an estimator
- know how to estimate proportions, means and totals from suitable samples
- be able to estimate the precision of an estimate
- know how to check that an estimator is unbiased
- know how to estimate the size of a population using a capture–recapture method
- know how to use the embarrassing question methods to estimate a proportion.

3

Design of experiments

Some people say that you can prove anything with statistics, but the truth of the matter is that you never prove anything with statistics.

A horticulturist has developed a new variety of potato which he claims gives higher yields than a standard variety with a similar taste. How could you test this claim?

The best way to test the claim is to undertake an *experiment*: to grow the two varieties and measure the yields. However, you need to design the experiment carefully. If you grow the standard variety in one field and the new variety in another, any difference in the yield per hectare may be due to differences in the soil quality, drainage or aspect of the fields. Even if you choose two plots of land which are identical as far as you can tell, and plant two sets of potatoes that are as alike as possible in terms of size and number, you do not expect to get exactly the same yield from each of them: there is some variability inherent in the situation.

In an experiment, some aspect of a situation is altered, and the effect of the alteration is measured. In this example, you (the experimenter) choose the plots, plant the varieties of potato and measure the yield. This is in contrast to a survey (such as an opinion poll), where the aim is simply to record the situation that exists without altering any aspect of it.

Often, organisations spend millions of pounds on the strength of experimental findings. The horticulturist may undertake a huge expansion of operations if your experiment confirms his claim. It is important that you are as certain as possible that the decision reached is the correct one. However, experiments themselves cost money: they need to be designed well so that
- the information obtained is reliable
- the maximum information is obtained for a specified cost (or the cost is minimised while obtaining the required information).

This chapter begins to look at the fundamental principles that should be followed when designing experiments. Some of them are analogous to principles that you met in Chapters 1 and 2 on surveys.

Principles of Experimental Design

Comparing like with like

In the potato example, it is clearly not satisfactory to plant one variety in one field and the other variety in another field: you are not then *comparing like with like*. A higher yield from the new variety might be due to differences in the fields rather than to the type of potato. The aim is to grow the two types of potato in situations that are as similar as possible. Ideally, the only thing that should differ is the type of potato.

For Discussion

There are many psychological experiments in which identical twins have been studied. Why do you think twins are of such interest to psychologists?

In any experiment there are sources of variability: it is virtually impossible to get exactly the same result from two successive experiments, even when the materials used and the conditions of the experiment are kept as constant as possible. Possible sources of variability are
- materials
- methods
- machines
- ambient conditions
- measuring instruments
- people.

Replication

For Discussion

If you had planted one half of a field with standard potatoes and the other half with the new variety, and the new variety produced the higher yield, would you accept that it was indeed better?

Again you should be wary. Even though using the same field means that you are trying to compare like with like, the higher yield might just be due to the inherent variability of the situation. It might not signify any real difference.

You need to know something about the variability of the yields from the two varieties in order to be able to make a valid comparison.To achieve this, you need to repeat or *replicate* the experiment several times. For example you might decide to divide the field into several plots, and allocate each variety to half of the plots. This would tell you something about the variability of each of the varieties under these conditions and so give you a much better idea of whether the two varieties were giving significantly different yields. Replication also allows you to estimate the variance of any statistical model that you develop from your results.

Randomisation

For Discussion

You have divided the field into 10 equal-sized plots in order to perform 5 replicate experiments. You suspect that some plots are more fertile than others because they are nearer to a stream or more sheltered from the wind. How will you decide which variety is to be sown in which plot?

Clearly there is a danger of introducing bias in a situation like this. Depending on your (possibly sub-conscious) prejudices, you might be tempted to put the new variety in the plots which you suspect to be more fertile, or perhaps to do exactly the opposite. The best solution is to randomise the allocation of the varieties to the plots. You could number the plots 0, 1, 2 ... , 9 and then write these numbers on identical pieces of paper, put them in a hat, shake it and then pull out five pieces of paper. The numbers written on the paper would be the plots in which you plant the new variety.

One real experiment that failed because the samples were not randomly chosen was a study into the benefits of free school milk. Initially the children who were to receive the free milk were chosen by some random method. Subsequently, teachers were told that they could move children from one group to another if the groups did not appear to be balanced in terms of social background. When it came to the analysis of the results, it was found that teachers had tended to move children from poorer backgrounds into the group that would receive free milk. As a result it was impossible to say whether differences between the two groups were due to the free milk or to social background. The two factors are said to have been *confounded* – their effects could not be separated.

Randomisation also makes it less likely that unknown factors will affect experimental results. In an experiment to see how the yield from a chemical reaction depends upon the concentration of one of the reagents, the experiments should not be performed in order of increasing concentration. It may be that some other effect, of which the experimenters are not aware, is going on at the same time. For example, the temperature of the room might be increasing. In this case, an increase in the yield might be due to the increasing temperature rather than to the change in the concentration of the reagent. (Of course, if temperature were known to be a problem, steps could be taken to control it.)

Randomisation requires the use of some kind of objective method for selecting a sample or choosing the sequence of tests. The choice of the sample must not be left to a human being, as it is easy to show that human beings frequently choose samples which are biased in some way, even when they are trying very hard to be fair. There are some experiments in which randomisation is quite obviously necessary, and others in which it does not appear to be required. However, it has been said that randomisation is analogous to insurance: the cost is usually relatively low, but it provides a safeguard against unforeseen disasters.

Pilot experiment

Unless you have previous experience of the proposed experiment, and know the possible problems and the sorts of measurements that are likely, it is wise to undertake a *pilot experiment*. This is a smaller version of the proposed experiment. It may identify problems that you have not envisaged, allowing you to improve the experimental design. It also enables you to estimate the amount of variability that should be expected in the response variable, so that you can decide how many replicates will produce a specified level of certainty in your conclusions.

Terminology

The standard term for a variable whose values are chosen by the experimenter is a *treatment*, or *factor*. The value of this variable is called its *level*. In some cases the level will be a number, such as the amount of fertiliser per square metre, and in others it will be a qualitative description. In the potato example, the 'treatment' is potatoes and the 'level' is the type of potato. The variable to be measured (the yield per hectare in the potato example) is called the *response variable*. The substance on which the treatment is used is called the *experimental material*: in the potato example, the field is the experimental material. An *experimental unit* is the smallest section of the experimental material which may receive a specific treatment. If the field were divided into plots in order to compare the yields from the potatoes, the plots would be the experimental units.

Blocks are sections of the experimental material which are assumed to differ from one another, but which are expected to be reasonably homogeneous within themselves. The fields could differ from each other in their location, in the amount and type of fertiliser applied in recent years, and/or in the effect of the crops grown in them in previous years. The variability within each block would generally be expected to be small compared with the variability between the blocks. There may, of course, be only one block, for example if all the plots were in the same field. Blocking is usually used when there is reason to expect variability between different sections of the experimental material. Randomisation, by contrast, should always be used, to minimise the effect of any unknown variability.

In the potato experiment, the aim is to make a comparison between two different treatments (the two varieties of potato). Sometimes you might wish instead to compare the effect of a treatment with the effect of no treatment. For example, you might wish to try out a fertiliser on a wheat crop. In order to see if it had any effect, you would need to leave some of the wheat unfertilised. The unfertilised wheat is called a *control*. It is actually common practice to include a control even when comparing several different treatments: an experiment to compare the effect of several different fuel additives on the fuel consumption of a car might well include a control run with no additive.

For Discussion

A manufacturer of noise-reducing screens for separating motorways from housing estates claims that her screen will reduce the noise level by 25%. She has chosen a motorway site where she can raise and lower a long section of screen fairly quickly. It takes about 5 minutes to raise or lower the screen and she leaves it in each position for about 10 minutes.

How would you run an experiment to test the claim? Identify which technical terms apply.

Dealing with subjective measurements

In the examples considered so far, the response variable can be measured. To measure the yield from the potatoes, the crop from each of the plots is simply weighed.

However, in an experiment to compare the durability of several kinds of paint exposed to severe weather conditions, the results may be in the form of an expert's assessment, by eye, of the finish of each paint at the end of the test period. If the expert has been involved in the development of the paints and already has ideas about which paint is best, this could lead to bias in the assessment. To avoid such bias, the experiment can be set up in such a way that the assessor does not know which paint is on which test square. This is one version of a *blind* experiment.

Another version of a blind experiment would be required to test a drug to prevent migraine headaches. If there are 30 migraine sufferers available for the test, 15 of these could be chosen at random and given the new treatment, whilst the remaining 15 could be given the standard treatment. Each person could be asked to record the number of migraine attacks that they had over a period of (say) 3 months. The migraine sufferers should be kept unaware of which treatment they are receiving, because there might be a tendency for those receiving the new treatment to feel better, just because they are receiving something which they perceive to be special.

An experiment is blind when the treatment used is unknown either to the subjects (experimental unit), or to the person making the assessment. In some cases, particularly in medical trials, a *double blind* experiment is used. In this case, both the patient receiving the treatment (the subject) and the person assessing the treatment are kept unaware of which treatment has been given to which patient.

It is well known that some patients get better just because they believe in the treatment. In medical trials, if a treatment is to be tested and no other treatment is available for comparison, a *placebo* may be given to the control group. A placebo is just a substance which has no healing effect, but which looks like the treatment which is being tested, so that patients cannot tell whether they are receiving treatment or not.

1. What are the advantages and disadvantages of each of the following methods for comparing two treatments for glandular fever?

    A   Ask several doctors to record for a year which of the treatments they give to glandular fever patients, and how quickly the patients recover.

    B   Ask the doctors to allocate patients to one or other of the treatments by spinning a coin (if it is heads, give treatment A, and if it is tails, give treatment B), and record how quickly they recover.

    C   Examine the records to find which patients had suffered from glandular fever during the last year, see which treatment they had been given and then ask the patients how long it took them to recover.

2. In each of the following cases, explain why the experiment does not compare like with like and suggest a better design for the experiment.

    A   A hi-fi salesman wishes to compare people's perception of the sound quality of a new system and a standard popular system. In order to do this, he asks 20 customers to listen first to the standard system and then to the new system, and to say which they prefer.

    B   A haulage firm is about to buy some new lorries and wishes to compare their performance. One aspect in which they are interested is the fuel consumption. To test this, they put one gallon of fuel into each of the lorries. Each lorry is then driven around a test track by a representative of the relevant manufacturer until the fuel is used up.

3. You are to design an experiment to test the effectiveness of two different toothpastes in reducing plaque. The assessment of the patients is to be done visually by a dentist, rather than using a measuring instrument. How would you organise the experiment?

4. A new formulation for relieving headaches is to be tested on a group of volunteers who suffer from frequent and severe headaches. The volunteers are to note down the severity of their headache and the time until they feel the relief from the medicine. The volunteers have been chosen partly on the basis that they all currently use the same dissolving tablet for relief from their headaches. How would you organise the experiment?

5. A precision engineering firm is deciding which of three suppliers to use for the carbide cutting inserts for one of their lathes. The lathe is used to produce pistons for a manufacturer of lorries. There is no difference in price between the three types of insert, so the criterion is to be the 'cutting edge life', defined as the number of pistons that can be produced before the surface of the pistons being produced becomes unsatisfactory. The cutting edge life of a single insert is expected to be about 200 pistons. A batch of material sufficient to test 5 inserts from each manufacturer is available.
    (i)   Why might it not be satisfactory to test all 5 inserts from manufacturer A, then all 5 from manufacturer B, then all 5 from manufacturer C?
    (ii) Why might it not be satisfactory to test 1 insert from manufacturer A, then 1 from manufacturer B, then 1 from manufacturer C, and so on?
    (iii) How would you decide on the order in which the inserts should be tested?

6. For each of the following experiments, identify (where relevant) the treatments, levels, experimental material, experimental

units, response variable, blocks and control.

A   An additive has just been developed to strengthen steel. One batch of molten steel is to be divided into 10 portions and the additive is to be put into 5 of them, which will be chosen at random.

B   A grower of soft fruit wishes to decide how much fertiliser she should use on her gooseberries to maximise their yield. There are 3 separate plots of gooseberries, and 6 rows in each plot. She wants to know whether to use a 'small' amount, a 'medium' amount or a 'large' amount of fertiliser, so she treats 2 rows in each plot with each of these amounts.

C   The Ministry of Defence wishes to compare two different tanks that might be purchased for the British Army. It is concerned about the reliability of the tanks and, in particular, wants to find out how much continuous use the army can expect from the tanks before any kind of repair is required. Tank teams are allocated at random to the tanks, and they are driven continuously around a large course, including firing at targets, until forced to stop for a repair.

D   An engineering firm needs a new drilling machine. It wishes to compare 3 types of machine. It has been decided that the machines will be judged on the number of holes that can be drilled in 10 minutes. There are 2 drills of each type, and workers are assigned at random to the drills. The material to be drilled is all taken from one large casting.

Fitting and checking models

Sometimes, the results of an experiment tell you immediately what you want to know. On other occasions, you might need to draw some simple plots and calculate the measures of location and spread. This *exploratory*, or *initial*, *data analysis* (*EDA* or *IDA*) is a very important part of the process of analysing experimental results, and may be all that is required. However, if the answer is not obvious, you may need to conduct a formal statistical hypothesis test in order to reach a decision. To conduct a hypothesis test it is often necessary to assume that the data may be satisfactorily modelled by a particular probability distribution, such as a Normal distribution.

For Discussion

Which model (binomial, Normal or Poisson) might you assume to be appropriate for each of these situations?
  A   The number of defective switches in a batch of 20.
  B   The lengths of pistons for a car engine.
  C   The number of accidents per month in a factory.
  D   The mean weight of samples of 5 bags of cement.
  E   The number of times per week that the drill bit breaks on a single machine.

Completely randomised design

Returning to the potato experiment, there would almost certainly be some variability in the fertility from one plot to another even if they were all in the same field. If you could measure this in some way, you could try to take it into account in the experimental design or in the model. However, if the fertility variations in the land were unknown, random allocation of the treatments would be the best you could do. An experiment in which there is only one block of experimental material, divided into units, and in which treatments are assigned to the units by some random method, is said to have a *completely randomised design*.

Suppose that the field could be divided into 10 plots and that 5 of them are chosen by some random method. The standard variety could be planted in these 5 plots, and the new variety could be planted in the remaining 5 plots.

Analysis of data from completely randomised experiments

Suppose that the potato experiment has now been done, using a completely randomised design. The arrangement of plots in the field and the yields per unit area, in suitable units, are as shown in figure 3.1.

S	S	N	S	N
(32)	(38)	(41)	(29)	(43)
N	S	N	N	S
(37)	(34)	(39)	(44)	(40)

S   standard variety

N   new variety

Yields per unit area given in brackets.

Figure 3.1

The results are summarised in the table and figure 3.2.

Yields of standard variety	Yields of new variety
29	37
32	39
37	40
38	41
40	43

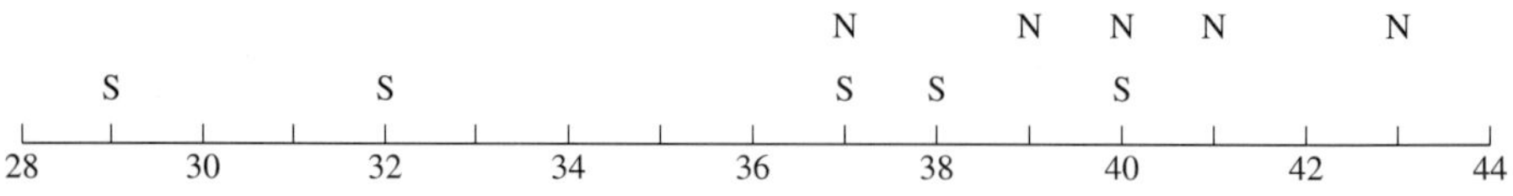

Figure 3.2

It does appear that the new variety tends to give higher yields, and possibly that its yields are more consistent. It would be worth carrying out further trials using the above results as a pilot experiment to decide how many replicates to use.

With more data, a box-plot or a back-to-back stemplot could be used to display the results. For a very large data set, a back-to-back histogram could be used (like a population pyramid). If more than two treatments are being compared, box-plots are still useful, but back-to-back stem-plots and histograms are not. Instead of back-to-back histograms, *comparative frequency polygons* can be used as in the next example. These are obtained by joining the midpoints of the tops of the columns in the histograms.

In many cases, these visual representations may be all that is required to make a decision.

EXAMPLE

In the hemming section of a clothing factory, the supervisor is interested in the effect of the material on the time which it takes one of the workers to perform his task. She arranges for the two materials of interest to be arranged in random order as they come to the machinist. The times taken for the task, in seconds, are given in the table below. The supervisor would have preferred to have used equal numbers of the two kinds of material, but this was not possible.

Material A	22.1	23.3	22.1	22.0	22.4	21.1	22.8	23.2	23.6
	26.2	20.7	21.1	22.3	21.6	20.6	22.2	23.1	
Material B	21.0	21.7	25.6	27.2	23.9	24.2	22.6	22.0	24.7
	26.4	21.9	23.3	22.0	22.9	22.4			

(i) Draw (a) a back-to-back stem-plot (b) a box-plot, (c) a back-to-back histogram and (d) frequency polygons for the data.
(ii) What conclusions can you draw?

Solution

(i)

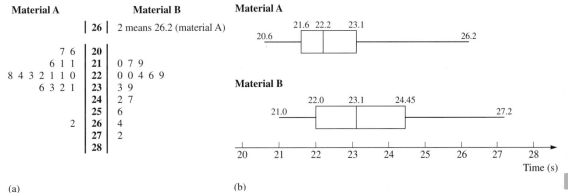

(a)

(b)

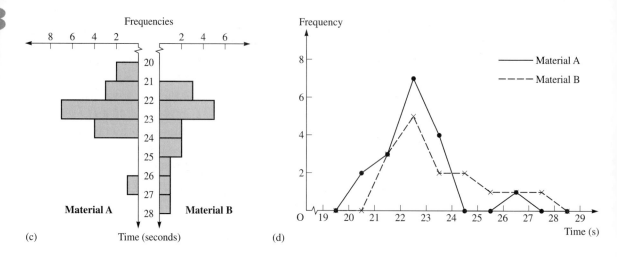

(c)

(d)

(ii) The machinist completes the task more quickly when working with material A, and there is also more variability with material B.

Sweeping by means

Sweeping by means is a very simple method of taking the investigation of data a little further. It may also be used in analysing more sophisticated experimental designs, as you will see later in this chapter.

The first step is to find the mean of each sample, and to use this as a summary of that sample. You then calculate the residual (observed value minus the mean) for each experimental unit. For the potato yield data, the results are as follows.

	Standard variety	New variety
Residuals	− 6.2 − 3.2 + 1.8 + 2.8 + 4.8	− 3 − 1 0 + 1 + 3
Mean	35.2	40

You can see from this that the new variety has a mean yield that is 4.8 units more than that of the standard variety. Whether this is a sufficiently large difference to convince you that the new variety really is better depends on the size of the residuals. In this case, the residuals are similar in size to the difference in the means, so the results are not particularly convincing.

In this situation the best thing to do would be to ask for further experiments to be done, using more replicates. The information from this first experiment could be used to estimate the variability expected in the results, and from this to suggest how many replicates to use. This initial experiment would effectively have been used as a pilot experiment.

3

With a large number of replicates (i.e. a large number of plots), you could use a z-test (because of the Central Limit Theorem – *Statistics 3*) to look for evidence of a real difference between the yields. With small data sets it might be appropriate to use the Mann-Whitney (two sample) test (*Statistics 4*) or possibly a two sample t-test.

Plots of the data will often be enough to indicate whether there is a difference between the treatments. Hypothesis tests may just be used to confirm the conclusions.

NOTE *There is a danger, especially when using a large number of replicates, that a hypothesis test will show a 'significant' difference even when that difference is too small to be of any practical importance. Statistically significant is not necessarily the same as practically important.*

In many situations, the number of replicates used is limited by practical considerations such as time and cost. For example, a farmer wishing to use only one field for the comparison of 3 types of wheat will want to use normal farm equipment to plant the crop. This will make very small plots impractical, and so limit the number of plots into which the fields may be divided. If an experiment involves using precious metals, or other expensive materials, the cost of a large number of replicates might be prohibitive. Some experiments in the chemical industry last for a week: if there is only one plant, it may only be possible to run one experiment at a time, so only a few replications of the experiment would be possible. In this case, time is the limiting factor.

Exercise 3B

1. A paint manufacturer wishes to test the durability of 4 different formulations for white paint. The plan is to apply the paints to 0.5 m square pieces of wood and to fix these along an outside wall of the factory. After one year the quality of the paint surface will be assessed by an expert. There are to be 7 replications for each formulation, so 28 squares of wood are required.
    (i)   Write a set of simple instructions so that a completely randomised design may be used to carry out this experiment.
    (ii) Explain the purpose of the design in this context.

2. In an experiment to assess the efficacy of a noise screen beside a motorway, 5 measurements were taken when the screen was up and another 5 were taken when the screen was down. The experiment was performed over a period when the traffic level was fairly constant and the times when the screen was up and down were chosen by random allocation.
    The following values were obtained.

Screen up	45	58	31	49	55
Screen down	83	71	76	65	74

    On the basis of the above values, would you accept the salesman's claim that this type of screen reduced the noise level by at least 25%?

Exercise 3B continued

3. The product development team at a paint factory has proposed that it would be better to use a bought-in resin in the paint than to use the resin produced in-house. In order to investigate whether the cost of this would be justified, an experiment is performed to test the resistance of the paint to a solvent. Paints containing the two different resins are randomly allocated to a total of 30 different surfaces, allowed to dry and then rubbed with solvent. The number of strokes required to disrupt the paint surface is taken as a measure of the solvent resistance of each paint. The results are given in the table below.

In-house	182 151 263 193 145 239 163 141
	112 177 122 117 157 160 135
Bought in	82 177 143 86 100 154 89 134
	112 80 104 120 90 118 107

Analyse these results and summarise your conclusions in a brief report.

4. A firm manufacturing light bulbs wishes to compare the effect of two gases (X and Y) which could be used to fill the bulbs, on the number of hours for which the bulbs may be used. In case there is some systematic variability in the quality of the bulbs being produced, a completely randomised design is used to assign each gas to 100 bulbs as they come from the production line. According to the Central Limit Theorem, the mean lifetimes should be approximately Normally distributed, and so should the difference in the means. The test statistic is

$$\frac{\bar{x} - \bar{y}}{\sqrt{\left(\dfrac{\hat{\sigma}_x^2}{50} + \dfrac{\hat{\sigma}_y^2}{50}\right)}}$$

The results of a completely randomised experiment are given in the table to the right.

Unfortunately, the original results are not available, only the summary statistics. Does there appear to be a significant difference between the effects of using the different gases? Can you say anything further?

Gas	Sample size	$\sum\limits_{i=1}^{50} x_i$	$\sum\limits_{i=1}^{50} (x_i - \bar{x})^2$
X	50	50 116	497 378
Y	50	52 062	280 794

5. In order to compare the yields from 4 varieties of wheat a completely randomised design is used with 5 replicates of each variety.

The resulting yields in kg ha^{-1} are shown in the table below.

Haven	Hereward	Hunter	Riband
7500	8300	7100	7500
8100	8000	7400	7500
7900	7800	7600	7700
7600	7900	7500	7400
7300	7400	7000	7100

(i) Assuming that the seeds for all the varieties cost the same amount, decide whether this experiment provides evidence of a significant difference between the varieties.

(ii) If the seed costs were not the same for each variety how would you modify your analysis to take this into account?

Paired design

For Discussion

You are planning an experiment to compare the two varieties of potato, and have been offered 10 small fields in different locations. The fields are too small to be split into more than two plots each. If you use a completely randomised design on the 10 fields (without splitting each one), the amount of variability from one field to another might well mask the differences between the varieties. If you split each of the fields into two plots and then use a completely randomised design, you still have the same problem.

How can you best organise the planting?

In this situation a *paired design* is appropriate. Each field is split into two plots, and then one plot in each field is randomly allocated to the new variety. The standard variety is planted in the other plot. The two plots in each field are likely to be similar, and so the differences in the yields should be due mainly to differences in the varieties. Since you have used random allocation to decide which plot in each field is planted with the new variety, you have avoided the problem of bias.

You can see that this is effectively a block design, but that in this case each block (field) contains only two experimental units (plots).

Manufacturers of soaps and detergents often use a paired design when they wish to compare the effect on customer's hands of a new product with that of a current product. They simply ask some volunteers to sit with one hand immersed in water containing the current product and the other hand in water containing the new product. The assumption is that the effect of the product on a person's right hand will be similar to the effect on the left hand, but it will probably be different from the effect on someone else's hands. As usual, the choice of which hand should be put in the new product should be done by a random method.

Analysis of data from paired experiments

In the experiment to compare the two varieties of potato, the results of the paired design are given in the following table.

Field	A	B	C	D	E	F	G	H	I	J
Yield from new variety	472	457	485	451	453	420	457	450	415	435
Yield from standard variety	470	451	483	450	452	418	452	451	416	437
Difference in yield (new– standard)	+ 2	+ 6	+ 2	+ 1	+1	+ 2	+ 5	− 1	− 1	− 2

Since the experiment has a paired design, it is useful to look at the differences in the yields for each field

From this it looks as if the new variety does give a larger yield. To analyse these results formally, you could use
- a sign test (see below),
- a Wilcoxon (one sample) ranked sum test (*Statistics 4*), or
- a (Student's) *t*-test (*Statistics 4*).

Your choice of test will depend on the assumptions you have made about the distribution of the yields.

The null hypothesis is that there is no difference between the varieties. The alternative hypothesis is that the new variety has a higher yield, so the test is one-tailed. A significance level of 5% is fairly standard.

For the sign test, the null hypothesis is that any differences between the yields are due to chance, so the probability that the new variety gives a higher yield than the standard variety is 0.5. The test statistic is the number of fields in which the new variety gives a higher yield than the standard variety. You model this by the random variable R, where

$$R \sim B(10, 0.5).$$

As the distribution of R is binomial, which is discrete, it is not possible to have a significance level of exactly 5%. From statistical tables you can obtain the following values.

$P(R \geq 8) = 0.0547 \qquad P(R \geq 9) = 0.0107 \qquad P(R = 10) = 0.0010.$

If you define the critical region as {9, 10}, the significance level is 0.0107 or 1.07%. If you define it as {8, 9, 10} the significance level is 0.0547 or 5.47%, which is close to the usual value of 5%. The critical region of {8, 9, 10} is clearly the best choice in this case.

In this case the test statistic, r, is 7. It does not fall in the critical region, so there is insufficient evidence to conclude that the new variety has a higher yield.

The working for the Wilcoxon test and the t-test is given in Appendix B. Both of these tests make assumptions about the distribution of the differences and it is important to check whether these assumptions are reasonable prior to using the tests. If their assumptions are valid then both of these tests are more powerful than the sign test (that is, they are more likely to detect a difference in the yields).

Sweeping by means in a paired experiment

You may use a version of the method of sweeping by means to find out more about the data obtained from the paired experiment on the two potato varieties.

The overall mean of the 20 yields is 448.75. Subtracting this from each of the yields in the table gives a table of residuals.

Field	A	B	C	D	E	F	G	H	I	J	
New variety residuals	23.25	8.25	36.25	2.25	4.25	−28.75	8.25	1.25	−33.75	−13.75	
Standard variety residuals	21.25	2.25	34.25	1.25	3.25	−30.75	3.25	2.25	−32.75	−11.75	
Column means	22.25	5.25	35.25	1.75	3.75	−29.75	5.75	1.75	−33.25	−12.75	448.75

The residuals tell you by how much the yield of each plot is above or below average. The mean of each column tells you by how much the yield of each field is above or below average. For example, the mean yield from Field A is 22.25 units above the overall average, with the new variety yielding 1 unit more than this and the standard yielding 1 unit less. You can rewrite the table to show the figures in this form.

Field	A	B	C	D	E	F	G	H	I	J	
New variety	+1	+3	+1	+0.5	+0.5	+1	+2.5	−0.5	−0.5	−1	
Standard variety	−1	−3	−1	−0.5	−0.5	−1	−2.5	+0.5	+0.5	+1	
Field effects	22.25	5.25	35.25	1.75	3.75	−29.75	5.75	1.75	−33.25	−12.75	448.75

This table shows clearly how the various fields compare, and how the two varieties of potato compare within each field. Fields A and C give the highest yields and F and I give the lowest. The main feature of interest, however, is that in 7 of the 10 fields the new variety produced a higher yield than the standard variety. Further, in the 3 fields in which the standard variety produced the higher yield, the differences were relatively small.

Sweeping by means has taken more time and effort than simply looking at the differences between the yields of the two varieties for each field, but it has also provided some extra information. In practical situations this extra information could well be worth the extra work. In some circumstances it provides sufficient information, and no further analysis is required. Usually, though, sweeping by means is used as a form of exploratory data analysis, to investigate data informally before going on to apply a formal hypothesis test.

Comparing several treatments

Whether you wish to compare 2 treatments or 22, you should always aim to follow the design principles of comparing like with like, randomisation and replication. Graphical methods of presenting the results are useful however many treatments are being compared. What may become less easy as the number of treatments increases is choosing a suitable hypothesis test.

You can use various tests to compare the treatments two at a time. The sign test, the one sample t-test, the Wilcoxon (one sample) test for paired data, the two sample t-test and the Mann-Whitney (two sample) test for unpaired data are all possibilities. However, there is a problem concerning the significance level.

Suppose that you wish to compare just three treatments, P, Q, and R. The null hypothesis is that all of the treatments are equivalent. To test this by comparing the treatments in pairs (P and Q, Q and R, P and R) using a significance level of 5%, you must perform three separate tests.

When the null hypothesis is correct,

$$P \text{ (reject the null hypothesis)} = P(\text{at least one of the tests gives a significant result})$$

$$= 1 - P \text{ (none of the tests gives a significant result)}$$

$$= 1 - 0.95^3$$

$$= 0.142625$$

This means that the probability of a *Type I Error* – rejecting the null hypothesis when it is correct – is about 14%. If you were comparing 22 treatments by testing them in pairs, the number of tests would be

$$^{22}C_2 = 231.$$

The overall significance level would be

$$1 - 0.95^{231} = 0.999\,992\,852.$$

In other words, you would almost certainly obtain some 'significant' results even if there were no differences between the treatments. If you try to compensate for this by reducing the significance level of the individual tests, the probability of a *Type II Error* – accepting the null hypothesis when it is false – is increased.

A way round this problem is to use the one-way "**An**alysis **Of V**ariance" (ANOVA) test (*Statistics 6*). The test is really just an extension of sweeping by means. For the test to be valid, each of the samples must be Normally distributed with the same variance. Inspection of the residuals reveals whether this is a reasonable assumption, and a probability plot can be used if required. If the assumptions required for ANOVA are not valid, then it may be appropriate to use a non-parametric (distribution-free) test instead.

Exercise 3C

1. A firm is about to update its computing facilities by buying a considerable number of new computers. Two models are being considered, and it is decided to compare these by seeing how long they take to carry out some standard spreadsheet and database operations. A paired design is used: each machine is made to perform the same operation on the same data using the same software. The results are shown in the following table.

Operation	A	B	C	D	E	F	G	H	I
Time on machine type X (s)	42.7	7.4	84.5	24.2	39.4	56.1	47.3	63.2	12.4
Time on machine type Y (s)	51.3	7.1	85.3	26.1	38.7	59.3	46.1	66.3	15.2

(i) Display these results on suitable charts and comment on them.
   (ii) Carry out
        (a) a sign test,
        (b) a Wilcoxon matched pairs rank sum test, and
        (c) a one sample t-test.
   Identify your assumptions in each case, and indicate whether they appear to be valid.
   (iii) State your conclusions and recommendations in a form suitable for the managers of the firm, who are not statisticians.

2. A laboratory needs to compare two methods for measuring the level of cholesterol in a person's blood. In order to do this a paired design is used: a sample of blood is taken from 20 people

and the cholesterol level in each sample is measured using the 2 different methods. The results are shown in the table below.

Subject	Method A	Method B
1	36.6	36.7
2	36.5	36.9
3	36.8	34.7
4	36.2	35.5
5	37.0	37.9
6	37.5	36.6
7	37.9	36.8
8	37.2	35.3
9	36.6	36.3
10	36.3	37.1
11	36.4	36.1
12	37.3	36.3
13	38.0	38.3
14	36.9	37.5
15	36.9	38.2
16	38.2	38.0
17	37.3	37.3
18	36.5	36.1
19	37.3	37.4
20	38.3	38.9

Analyse these results to see if there is any difference between the two methods.

3. The resistance to solvents of a paint can be tested by rubbing the paint surface with a solvent-soaked pad, and counting the number of rubs required to disrupt the surface coating. A paint manufacturer is considering changing the type of resin it puts into its paints, and wants to compare the solvent-resistance of the resulting paint to that of the current formula.

CIS

Exercise 3C continued

Since the results may depend upon the surface to which the paint is applied, 15 different surfaces are prepared and each paint is applied to half of each surface, random allocation being used to specify which half is used for which paint. The results are given in the table below.

Surface	Resin A	Resin B
A	182	173
B	151	154
C	263	255
D	193	186
E	145	147
F	239	221
G	163	161
H	141	145
I	112	118
J	177	153
K	122	122
L	117	114
M	157	149
N	160	155
O	135	128

Use a graphical method to analyse the differences between the two kinds of paint. What conclusion do you reach and what would be your recommendation to the management?

The technical director asks you to confirm your assessment with a hypothesis test. Use a non-parametric test and explain briefly why a *t*-test would not be appropriate in this case.

(The situation here is similar to that in question 3 in exercise 3B, but notice that the experimental design is different.)

4. Researchers at a detergent factory are developing new products for the washing of protective clothing badly soiled by industrial waste. Five products have reached the stage of comparative trials and an experiment is to be designed for this purpose. Typical washing loads will be washed by the new products and assessed for cleanliness.
   (i)   (a) What is the purpose of replication?
         (b) How could the principle of replication be applied in this experiment?
   (ii) (a) What is the purpose of randomisation?
         (b) How could the principle of randomisation be applied in this experiment?
   (iii) What practical problems might arise in organising this experiment?

Randomised block design

A grower of soft fruit wishes to compare 4 different fertilisers (W, X, Y, Z) to see which gives the highest yield. She has 3 small fields (A, B, C) available for the experiment. She knows from past experience that the fields differ in fertility, but she does not have any records to quantify this. The fertiliser sprayer is sufficiently small that each field can be divided into 12 sections and a different fertiliser applied to each. The fertilisers are allocated to the sections using random allocation, and the resulting layout is shown in figure 3.3. This is an example of a randomised block design.

Field A
W	W	Y
X	Z	X
Z	Y	Y
X	Z	W

Field B
X	W	Z
Y	W	X
Y	Z	Z
W	X	Y

Field C
Y	X	W
W	Z	Y
Z	W	X
X	Y	Z

Figure 3.3

Using each fertiliser within each field enables the grower to separate the effects of the field fertilities from the effects of the fertilisers. A randomised block design is actually an extension of a paired design: in this case the fields are the blocks, and instead of 2 treatments (as in a paired experiment), each field receives 4 different treatments. As for paired designs, the allocation of the treatments (the fertilisers) within each block is done using random numbers.

Each fertiliser is used on 3 sections of each field. There are therefore 3 replicates of each treatment within each block, and so it is possible to assess the variability within the blocks for each fertiliser. In this example, each block has the same number of replicates of each treatment: the design is said to be *balanced*. If the number of replicates varies from block to block, the design is said to be *unbalanced*.

Balanced designs are generally preferred, since the analysis turns out to be a little simpler. However, in some situations unbalanced designs are unavoidable because of the nature of the blocks. For example, suppose that you wish to try out three different treatments on the salmon tanks on a fish farm. Each tank is already divided into 8 separate sections. Taking the tanks as the blocks, you can either use only two replicates of each treatment per block (leaving 2 sections in each block unused) or use an unbalanced design.

Analysis of data from randomised block experiments

A good first step in analysing the results of a randomised block experiment is to look at simple data displays. The conclusion might be obvious from this initial data analysis. It might be helpful to calculate the means and, possibly, some measure of spread. However, a more formal analysis is quite complicated when there are several replicates per block. The formal analysis usually involves the method of *Analysis of Variance (Statistics 6)* which requires that the response variable should be Normally distributed and that the variance should be the same within each block.

When each treatment is used exactly once in each block, the situation is simpler, and can be analysed in several straightforward ways.

Another fruit farmer wishing to compare the effects of the 4 fertilisers has 7 fields (A, B, C, D, E, F and G) available for his experiment. In this case, however, it is only possible to divide each field into 4 plots. The arrangement is shown in figure 3.4.

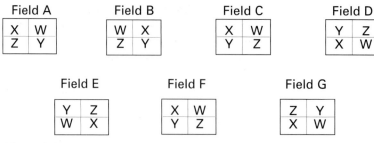

Field A

X	W
Z	Y

Field B

W	X
Z	Y

Field C

X	W
Y	Z

Field D

Y	Z
X	W

Field E

Y	Z
W	X

Field F

X	W
Y	Z

Field G

Z	Y
X	W

Figure 3.4

The resulting yields are given in the table below.

	Treatment (Fertiliser)			
Field	**W**	**X**	**Y**	**Z**
A	53	54	56	60
B	59	62	68	71
C	36	39	39	41
D	49	51	58	59
E	53	58	69	75
F	35	35	36	39
G	66	67	69	76

It is clear without further analysis in this case that the yields increase from W to X to Y to Z in each field, and so this is the order of effectiveness of the fertilisers. Sometimes the effects of the treatments may not be as clear as this, and you need to investigate the results a little further. The technique of sweeping by means may be helpful.

Sweeping by means in a randomised block experiment

As before, you start by calculating the mean yield for each field, then subtract this from each of the observed yields. For example, the mean yield for field A is

$$\tfrac{1}{4}(53 + 54 + 56 + 60) = 55.75.$$

When fertiliser W is applied the yield for field A is 53: this is 2.75 units less than the average for Field A:

$$53 - 55.75 = -2.75.$$

Subtracting the field mean from each individual result in this way gives the following table.

Block (fields)	Treatment (Fertiliser)				Block effect
	W	X	Y	Z	
A	−2.75	−1.75	+0.25	+4.25	55.75
B	−6	−3	+3	+6	65
C	−2.75	+0.25	+0.25	+2.25	38.75
D	−5.25	−3.25	+3.75	+4.75	54.25
E	−10.75	−5.75	+5.25	+11.25	63.75
F	−1.25	−1.25	−0.25	+2.75	36.25
G	−3.5	−2.5	−0.5	+6.5	69.5

This table shows how much each yield was above or below the average for the field. You can see, for example, that the yields from plots treated with fertiliser W are always below average, and those from plots treated with fertiliser Z are always above average.

It is possible to go one stage further, by applying a similar process to the columns, including the 'block effect' column, giving the table below. (The figures are all given correct to 2 decimal places.)

> The mean of the column for W is − 4.61: you put this at the bottom of the column and change the first entry in the column to + 1.86, since − 2.75 is 1.86 above this column mean

Block	Treatment (Fertiliser)				Block effect
	W	X	Y	Z	
A	+1.86	+0.71	−1.43	−1.14	+1
B	−1.39	−0.54	+1.32	+0.61	+10.25
C	+1.86	+2.71	−1.43	−3.14	−16
D	−0.64	−0.79	+2.07	−0.64	−0.5
E	−6.14	−3.29	+3.57	+5.86	+9
F	+3.36	+1.21	−1.93	−2.64	−18.5
G	+1.11	−0.04	−2.18	+1.11	+14.75
Treatment effect	−4.61	−2.46	+1.68	+5.39	+54.75

The effect of this process is to decompose each of the original values into the sum of four components. For example, the top left entry in the table can be broken down as

Observed value = overall mean + block effect + treatment effect + residual

$$53 \quad = \quad 54.75 \quad + \quad 1 \quad + \quad -4.61 \quad + \quad 1.86$$

By using this process you are effectively fitting an *additive model* to the data. The assumption is that the actual yield is the sum of
- an overall mean
- a block (field) effect
- a treatment (fertiliser) effect and
- a residual.

The residuals should be the result of random elements. If there is some pattern in the residuals, the validity of this assumption should be checked. In this example, there is no noticeable pattern.

For Discussion

Why would the existence of some pattern in the residuals make you doubt the suitability of an additive model?

The size of the residuals is the standard against which the differences between the treatments are measured. If the differences between the treatment effects are large compared to the residuals, it seems likely that there is a real difference between the treatments. If the differences between the treatment effects are similar to (or smaller than) the residuals, they could just be a result of the variability of the situation.

You can use various types of plot to look at the residuals. A dot-plot can be used when the samples are very small. A stem-plot is helpful for larger samples. A box-plot is more useful for very large samples.

For the fruit-growing example, the stem-plot is given in figure 3.5 (a). Remember that the numbers in a stem-plot are usually cut rather than rounded: the 1.86 in the table is entered as 1.8 and not as 1.9. (This makes it easier to find the corresponding value in a data list when you wish to query a particular entry on a stem-plot.) However, as this is only an exploratory data analysis it doesn't really matter whether you cut or round.

Figure 3.5 (b) shows the *five letter summary* of the residuals. The summary contains the five values that are required to draw the box-plot. The *hinge spread* (*inter-quartile range*) and the range have been shown to the right of the summary.

The box-plot of the residuals is shown in figure 3.5 (c). The 'whiskers' of the box-plot extend only as far as observations which are not outliers. (When working with the median and the hinges, an outlier is usually defined as an observation which is more than $1\frac{1}{2}$ times the hinge spread beyond one of the hinges. An extreme outlier is an observation which is more than 3 times the hinge spread beyond one of the hinges.)

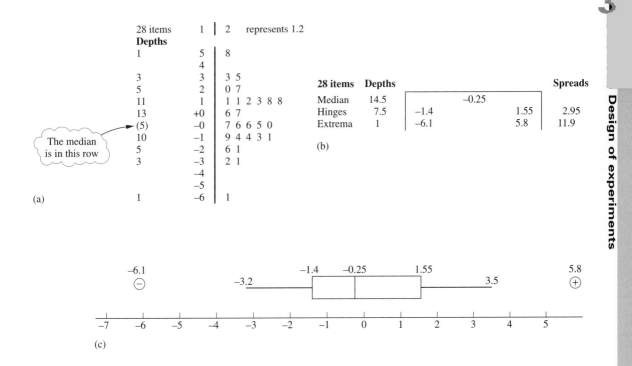

Figure 3.5

The reason for looking at the residuals was to see whether the differences between the fertilisers, found using the method of sweeping by means, represented real differences or whether they might just be due to random variability. If the additive model is appropriate, the random variation is given by the residuals. The shape of the stem-plot suggests that a Normal distribution may be appropriate to model the residuals. Most of the residuals lie between −3.2 and +3.5, a range of 6.7. Therefore it is reasonable to accept that differences greater than 6.7 represent real differences. Using this criterion, it appears that fertiliser Z really is better than both W and X since the difference between the treatment effects for Z and W is 10 (5.39 + 4.61) and the difference between the treatment effects for Z and X is 7.85 (5.39 + 2.46). The other differences may just be due to experimental variability.

The standard method of analysis for randomised block designs is *two-way ANOVA* (Analysis of Variance). This is an extension of the technique of sweeping by means. For the hypothesis tests in two-way ANOVA to be valid, the additive model should fit the data and the residuals should be Normally distributed with the same variance. This can be checked by looking at the tables obtained by sweeping by means, and using a probability plot if necessary.

Design of experiments

Activity

Show that the same decomposition of the above data is obtained by the following alternative method.

1. Calculate the overall mean and subtract this from all of the values in the table.
2. Calculate the means of each row and column to obtain the row and column effects.
3. Subtract the row and column effects from the values in the table obtained at step 1 to find the residuals.

(This method is slightly quicker than sweeping by means, but sweeping by means leads on more naturally to median polish, covered below.)

Median polish

Resistant statistics

In a small sample, the presence of one exceptionally large value will have a considerable effect on both the mean and the standard deviation. If the exceptional value can be shown to be an error, then it may be discarded. Otherwise, you should be very wary of discarding it. One sensible approach is to do the analysis twice: once including the value and once excluding it. If the conclusion is unchanged, then there is no need to worry. If the conclusions are different, it may be necessary to obtain more data.

Because of this problem, it is sometimes better to work with *resistant statistics*. These are measures of location and spread which are affected little, if at all, by extreme values in the data. The median and the inter-quartile range are examples of resistant statistics.

Suppose that the 5 measurements taken in an experiment were

12.3   13.8   15.7   15.9   16.5,   Mean 14.84, median 15.7
SD = 1.59, IQR = 2.1

but that by mistake, they were recorded as

12.3   13.8   15.7   15.9   **165**.   Mean 44.54, median 15.7
SD = 60.24, IQR = 2.1

You can see that the mean and the standard deviation are significantly affected by the error, whereas the median and the inter-quartile range are unaffected. In this case the error might easily be detected and the value corrected or discarded. However, in other cases an extreme value might be correct or it might not be detected. In such cases, the use of the median gives a measure of location which is much more stable and, arguably, much more representative of the data set. The median and the inter-quartile range are called resistant statistics because they are resistant to the effects of outliers, or extreme values.

Median polish is a method similar to sweeping by means. It is resistant to outliers, and is easier to perform by hand. The aim is the same: to fit an additive model to the data.

To see how the method works, look again at the data from the comparison of 4 different fertilisers used on 7 different fields (below).

The first step is to find the row (block) medians.

| Block | Treatment (Fertiliser) | | | | Block |
	W	X	Y	Z	median
A	53	54	56	60	55
B	59	62	68	71	65
C	36	39	39	41	39
D	49	51	58	59	54.5
E	53	58	69	75	63.5
F	35	35	36	39	35.5
G	66	67	69	76	68

This tells you that field G gave the best overall yields and that field F was the worst overall.

The next step is to subtract the row medians from the values in the rows.

| Block | Treatment (Fertiliser) | | | | Block |
	W	X	Y	Z	median
A	−2	−1	+1	+5	55
B	−6	−3	+3	+6	65
C	−3	0	0	+2	39
D	−5.5	−3.5	+3.5	+4.5	54.5
E	−10.5	−5.5	+5.5	+11.5	63.5
F	−0.5	−0.5	+0.5	+3.5	35.5
G	−2	−1	+1	+8	68

At this stage you can easily compare the performances of the different fertilisers within each field. As before, the yields obtained using fertiliser W are always below average (the median in this case) and those obtained using fertiliser Z are always above average.

You now find each of the column medians. In the fertiliser columns this is the average amount by which the yield is above or below the median value for the field. In the final column, it is the overall average (median) yield.

Commercial and industrial statistics

Block	Treatment (Fertiliser)				Block median
	W	X	Y	Z	
A	−2	−1	+1	+5	55
B	−6	−3	+3	+6	65
C	−3	0	0	+2	39
D	−5.5	−3.5	+3.5	+4.5	54.5
E	−10.5	−5.5	+5.5	+11.5	63.5
F	−0.5	−0.5	+0.5	+3.5	35.5
G	−2	−1	+1	+8	68
Column median	−3	−1	+1	+5	+55

You can now see clearly that fertiliser Z gives the highest yields overall – on average it is 4 units better than Y, 6 units better than X and 8 units better than W.

Finally, you subtract each column median from each value in the corresponding column.

Block	Treatment (Fertiliser)				Block median
	W	X	Y	Z	
A	+1	0	0	0	0
B	−3	−2	+2	+1	+10
C	0	+1	−1	−3	−16
D	−2.5	−2.5	+2.5	−0.5	−0.5
E	−7.5	−4.5	+4.5	+6.5	+8.5
F	+2.5	+0.5	−0.5	−1.5	−19.5
G	+1	0	0	+3	+13
Column median	−3	−1	+1	+5	+55

The significance of the results depends how they compare with the residuals in the table. If the differences between the treatment medians are large compared with the residuals then the differences are probably important. If the residuals are large compared with the differences between the treatment medians, the differences are probably not significant.

A dot-plot, or a stem-plot, of the residuals enables us to look at their distribution (figure 3.6).

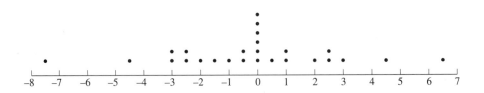

Figure 3.6

Most of the residuals lie between −3 and +2.5, which is a range of 5.5. This means that fertiliser Z does seem to be significantly better than W and X because its effect is greater by 8 units (5 + 3) and 6 units (5 + 1), respectively. The other treatment differences are of the same magnitude as the residuals and could therefore be due to the natural variability of the situation.

NOTE	*Unlike sweeping by means, median polish gives different results if you start with the columns rather than the rows. It makes sense to start with the blocks, to remove their effect, and then move on to the treatments, as in the example above. If the median of the row medians or the column medians is not zero, the whole process may be repeated.*

Exercise 3D

1. The table below shows the results for a different set of fertilisers. Use either version of sweeping by means to analyse them. Summarise your findings in a brief report.

Block	Treatment (Fertiliser)			
	P	Q	R	T
A	48	58	65	75
B	54	62	75	83
C	58	70	78	93
D	68	73	83	102
E	68	83	97	108
F	74	88	101	116
G	77	94	104	122

2. In an experiment to compare the yields from different varieties of wheat, a randomised block design was used. The results are given in the table below. Analyse the results and write a short report summarising any differences between the yields of the varieties.

Block	Variety			
	Haven	Hereward	Hunter	Riband
1	7500	8300	7100	7500
2	8100	8000	7400	7500
3	7900	7800	7600	7700
4	7600	7900	7500	7400
5	7300	7400	7000	7100

3. A company is about to buy some new machines for making widgets on a

production line. It is considering 3 different types of machine (A, B and C), all costing approximately the same amount. In order to help in the decision process, 5 operators (P, Q, R, S and T) from the production line are asked to try out each of the 3 machines. The operators are allocated to the machines in a random order, and then given time to familiarise themselves with the machine before seeing how many widgets they can produce in one hour.

Case 1
One possible set of results is given in the table below.

Operator	Machine		
	A	B	C
P	72	74	79
Q	77	84	88
R	59	59	67
S	44	51	61
T	41	49	58

Case 2
Another possible set of results is shown below.

Operator	Machine		
	A	B	C
P	82	74	73
Q	77	91	78
R	62	50	67
S	34	51	64
T	35	49	68

(i) Look at both tables. Do you feel confident to make a decision straight away in either of the cases?

(ii) Analyse both sets of results using median polish.

(iii) State in each case which machine should be purchased on the basis of these results (assuming that no further tests can be done). In each case say how certain you feel about your conclusion.

4. Wheat responds well to applications of nitrogen fertiliser. Because of environmental concerns, this is applied in a number of separate applications (*top dressings*). Even when the total amount of fertiliser is kept constant, changing the timing of the top dressings can affect the growth of the crop. In an experiment to compare the effect of different top-dressing patterns on one particular variety of wheat (Hereward), a randomised block design was used. The yields in kg ha^{-1} are given in the table below.

Block	Pattern of application		
	X	Y	Z
1	8300	8500	8800
2	8000	8400	8700
3	7800	8200	8000
4	7900	7900	8500
5	7400	8400	8000

(i) Use median polish to analyse these results.

(ii) Report your conclusions.

The following year the experiment was repeated using a different variety of wheat (Hunter). The yields in kg ha^{-1} were as follows.

Block	Pattern of application		
	X	Y	Z
1	7100	7400	7900
2	7400	7900	8200
3	7600	7500	8100
4	7500	7500	7900
5	7000	8000	7300

(iii) Use median polish again to analyse these results. Are your conclusions the same as for the Hereward?

5. In an experiment to compare the effects of different forms of lighting on the number of eggs laid by hens, a randomised block design was used. Each block consisted of a pen of 6 hens. One of the 3 treatments was natural light, and the other two involved extending 'daylight' hours using low intensity and high intensity light respectively. The yields (number of eggs in twelve weeks) are given in the table below.

Block	Treatment		
	Natural	High	Low
1	330	372	359
2	288	340	337
3	295	343	373
4	313	341	302

Use a suitable method to analyse these results and report your conclusions.

6. Researchers at a detergent factory are developing 5 experimental products for the washing of protective clothing badly soiled by industrial waste. The products have reached the stage of comparative trials and an experiment is to be designed for this purpose. Typical loads will be washed using each of the products, and assessed for cleanliness.

(i) High capacity washing machines suitable for heavy-duty washing are made by 5 manufacturers. The researchers can carry out 50 experimental washes. Explain why a randomised block design, with the machines as the blocks, would be more sensible for the allocation of the experimental washes to the products, than a completely randomised design.

(ii) In a preliminary investigation each product was used once in each machine. The results are shown in the table in the form of a standard cleanliness measure determined for each wash. Use two complete steps of median polish to analyse these data.

Product	Machine				
	1	**2**	**3**	**4**	**5**
A	31	23	45	25	27
B	21	14	36	16	19
C	17	17	27	31	35
D	18	21	27	32	38
E	26	21	36	31	32

(iii) Use the results of the median polish to explain
   (a) the advantages of using the randomised block design in the full experiment, and
   (b) whether you feel that the randomised block experiment will be sufficient.

Cross-over designs

Sixteen suitable patients suffering from a particular condition have been identified for a clinical trial to compare two different treatments. One approach is to use a completely randomised design: this would mean dividing the patients (at random) into two groups of 8, administering one treatment to each of the groups, and looking at the mean response for each group. If the effect of the treatment varied considerably from person to person, there would be quite a lot of variability in the final results.

An alternative approach is to use a *cross-over design*. Cross-over experiments are often used when there is only a small amount of experimental material available: in clinical trials this means when there is only a small number of suitable patients available. A cross-over design uses the same experimental material twice: each experimental unit receives first one treatment then another. In this case one group of 8 patients would receive treatment A first, and the other would receive treatment B first. Then the experiment would be repeated with the treatments the other way round (hence the term 'cross-over'). The design is represented in the diagram in figure 3.7. It is effectively a paired design, in which each experimental unit is paired with itself. Any differences in the response variable should be due to the treatments rather than to variations in the experimental material.

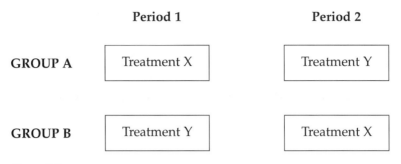

	Period 1	**Period 2**
GROUP A	Treatment X	Treatment Y
GROUP B	Treatment Y	Treatment X

Figure 3.7

Such an arrangement would enable you to see the differences between the treatments for each person, rather than just an aggregated result for a group of people, but there are some pitfalls.

For Discussion

What major problem do you foresee with a cross-over design?

You probably realised that there is a danger of *carry-over effects* when a cross-over design is used. A patient who has already received one treatment may react differently to the second treatment because of some longer-term effect of the first. To minimise carry-over effects, cross-over designs usually allow a flushing out period between the two treatments, to try to allow time for the effect of the first treatment to be removed from the experimental units. It is possible to estimate the effect of any remaining carry-over effects during the analysis of the results.

Analysis of data from cross-over experiments

In a cross-over experiment to compare a new variety of potato with the standard variety grown in a particular region, a field was divided into 10 plots. The standard variety was randomly allocated to 5 of these for the first year and the new variety was grown in the remaining 5 plots. In the second year, the plots which had been used for the standard variety were used for the new variety, and vice versa.

The arrangement, and the yields in kg (per plot of area 200 m²) are shown in figure 3.8.

Year 1

New (533)	Standard (508)	New (526)	New (553)	Standard (434)
New (467)	Standard (446)	New (534)	Standard (480)	Standard (487)

Standard (454)	New (554)	Standard (441)	Standard (465)	New (478)
Standard (379)	New (497)	Standard (452)	New (526)	New (537)

Figure 3.8

For Discussion

Can you draw any conclusions directly from the tables above?

Calculating the difference for each plot (yield for new variety minus yield for standard variety) produces the following results.

Increase in yield using the new variety

+79	+46	+85	+88	+44
+88	+51	+82	+46	+50

It is obvious that the new variety does increase the yield. The mean increase is 65.9 and the standard deviation is 18.8 (to 3 significant figures). Formal hypothesis tests are not required: there is a clear difference between the two varieties.

You may also have noticed that there appears to be a difference between the plots where the new variety was grown in the first year and where it was grown in the second year.

Increase in yield obtained using the new variety in the first year

+79		+85	+88	
+88		+82		

Increase in yield obtained using the new variety in the second year

	+46			+44
	+51		+46	+50

CIS

Design of experiments

For the plots where the new variety was grown in the first year, the new variety shows a mean improvement on the old variety of 84.4, with a standard deviation of 3.5 (to 1 decimal place), whereas for the plots where the new variety was grown in the second year, the new variety shows a mean improvement on the old variety of only 47.7, with a standard deviation of 2.7 (to 1 decimal place).

For Discussion

Suggest at least two possible explanations for this result.

Exercise 3E

1. In each of the following cases say why a cross-over design would, or would not, be appropriate. If you do not believe that a cross-over design is appropriate try to suggest an alternative.

(a) A poultry farmer wishes to compare the effects of two different diets on the weights of eggs produced by her hens. The hens are kept in ten different buildings and all of the hens in each building must have the same diet.

(b) A manufacturer of sports clothing wishes to compare the effects on the work rate of the employees of playing local radio over the PA system or playing uninterrupted music. The employees work in six different large rooms which are sufficiently separated from each other so that whatever is played over the PA system in one room will not be heard in the others.

(c) A large software house wishes to compare two different methods of teaching employees to program in the language C++. There are about 50 employees who currently need to learn C++. Afterwards, new employees who do not already know the language will be taught by whichever method is identified as the better by the experiment.

(d) A pharmaceutical firm wishes to test two treatments for alleviating the symptoms of a fairly rare disease. Only 10 patients are currently available to try the treatments.

2. A large clothing manufacturer is about to replace all of its sewing machines. Following initial research, the choice has been narrowed to two similarly-priced machines. The suppliers of the machines have agreed to lend 5 machines of each type to the manufacturer for 1 day of trials.

A cross-over experiment is conducted, in which 10 employees are chosen and then allocated at random to the 2 types of machine (P and Q). They are given half an hour to familiarise themselves with the machines, then the number of items they produce in the next hour is recorded. They are then given a break before repeating the procedure on the other type of machine. The results are shown in the tables below.

First trial

Worker	1	2	3	4	5	6	7	8	9	10
Machine	P	Q	P	Q	Q	P	Q	P	P	Q
No. produced	29	20	21	17	14	25	14	10	25	24

Second trial

Worker	1	2	3	4	5	6	7	8	9	10
Machine	Q	P	Q	P	P	Q	P	Q	Q	P
No. produced	23	19	14	21	17	16	15	13	17	22

(i) Which machine should the clothing manufacturer buy?
(ii) Do you notice anything of further interest in the results?

KEY POINTS

When you have worked through this chapter you should
- understand the importance of replication and randomisation
- understand the terms *treatment, factor, response variable, experimental material, experimental unit, block, control, placebo, blind (and double blind) experiment, resistant statistics*
- understand when and how to use completely randomised and randomised block experimental designs
- be able to analyse, using sweeping by means or median polish, the results of completely randomised and randomised block experiments
- understand when and how to use paired and cross-over experiments
- be able to analyse the results of paired and cross-over experiments.

Latin squares and factorial designs

Statistically significant is not the same as practically important.

The rate at which hemming can be done depends upon the sewing machine used, the type of fabric being sewn and the skill of the operator.

A textile company needs to compare the speed of 4 types of sewing machine in order to decide which type to purchase. The fabric sewn at the factory falls into 4 clear categories. The company has arranged to borrow one machine of each type for the first week in March. All the necessary information must be gathered in that week.

How should the experiment be conducted?

The response variable in this situation is the number of items hemmed in one day. The treatments are the 4 sewing machines. If enough information could be gathered during the week using only 1 operator, a randomised block design could be used, with each type of fabric constituting a block of experimental material.

However, since an operator can only work on one machine at a time, this would mean that 3 machines would be lying idle. In order to gather as much information as possible, it would be better to use 4 operators, so that all 4 machines could be in use all week. If there were only 1 type of fabric, a randomised block design could then be used, with each operator constituting a block.

The problem is that in this situation (and in many others) the experimental material is classified in two different ways — in this case the operators and the types of material. You need a new type of experimental design: a *Latin square* design.

Latin squares

The organisation of the Latin square for the hemming experiment is shown in the following table. The operators are called A, B, C and D; the fabric types are called P, Q, R, and S; the machines are called 1, 2, 3 and 4. The essential feature is that each machine is used once by each operator and once on fabric of each type.

Operator

Fabric type		A	B	C	D
	P	1	2	3	4
	Q	4	1	2	3
	R	3	4	1	2
	S	2	3	4	1

To use a Latin square design, you need the number of blocks under each classification (the number of operators and the number of fabric types in this case) to be the same as the number of treatments. Because there are 4 machines to be tested, the company must use 4 operators and 4 types of fabric.

Latin squares are used in situations like this where there are three variables. The analysis will give information about the differences between the machines, the differences between the operators and also the effects of the different fabrics. The company may be interested in all of this information, or just in the differences between the machines.

Activity

Use your calculator or random number tables to choose four pairs of numbers, each number between 1 and 4. Starting with the Latin square above, exchange the two rows identified by your first pair of numbers, then the two columns given by your second pair of numbers, then the two rows given by your third pair of numbers and, finally, the two columns identified by your final pair of numbers.

Check that the arrangement which remains is still a Latin square.

This method may be used to produce new Latin Square designs from the basic design.

How many different Latin squares of size 4 can you make?

Analysis of data from Latin square experiments

The numbers of items hemmed are given in the following table.

Operator

Fabric type		A	B	C	D
	P	910	980	1100	1310
	Q	1180	870	1040	1160
	R	1150	1280	970	1130
	S	1100	1150	1300	990

To see which result goes with which machine you need to refer back to the original table.

The Latin square has provided a way of organising the experiment. Now a version of sweeping by means (the version used in the Activity on page 66) will be used to investigate these data. The first step is to find the *overall* (or *grand*) mean and to subtract it from all of the values in the table. The results of this are shown below.

Operator

Fabric type		A	B	C	D
	P	−191.25	−121.25	−1.25	+208.75
	Q	+78.75	−231.25	−61.25	+58.75
	R	+48.75	+178.75	−131.25	+28.75
	S	−1.25	+48.75	+198.75	−111.25

1101.25

This is the overall mean

The next step is to estimate the operator effects, by finding the mean of each column; the fabric effects, by finding the mean of each row; and the machine effects, by finding the mean of the entries for each machine.

In this case, the entries for machine 1 all appear on the 'leading diagonal' of the original square. The mean effect of loom 1 is therefore

$$\frac{1}{4}(-191.25 - 231.25 - 131.25 - 111.25) = -\frac{665}{4} = -166.25$$

Performing all of these sets of calculations gives the tables below.

Operator   **Operator effects**

Fabric type		A	B	C	D	
	P	−191.25	−121.25	−1.25	+208.75	−26.25
	Q	+78.75	−231.25	−61.25	+58.75	−38.75
	R	+48.75	+178.75	−131.25	+28.75	+31.25
	S	−1.25	+48.75	+198.75	−111.25	+33.75
Fabric effects		−16.25	−31.25	+1.25	+46.25	1101.25

Machine	1	2	3	4
Effect	−166.25	−38.75	+38.75	+166.25

Notice that the sum of each set of effects is zero (a useful check).

Sweeping by means has decomposed each of the original entries by assuming an additive model. For the top left entry, which applies to Operator A working on machine 1 with fabric type A,

observed value = overall mean + operator effect + fabric effect + machine effect + residual.

$$910 = 1101.25 + (-16.25) + (-26.25) + (-166.25) + 17.5$$

As usual when using the method of sweeping by means, the size of the residuals indicates whether the differences between the machines are likely to be real or just part of the natural variability in the situation. To find the residuals you subtract the operator effect, the fabric effect and the machine effect from each value in the table, giving the results below.

		Operator				Operator effects
		A	B	C	D	
Fabric type	P	+17.5	−25	−15	+22.5	−26.25
	Q	−32.5	+5	+15	+12.5	−38.75
	R	−5	+12.5	+2.5	−10	+31.25
	S	+20	+7.5	−2.5	−25	+33.75
Fabric effects		−16.25	−31.25	+1.25	+46.25	1101.25

A stem-plot of the residuals is given in figure 4.1.

```
1 | 2    represents 12

+2 | 0 2
+1 | 2 2 5 7
+0 | 2 5 7
-0 | 5 2
-1 | 5 0
-2 | 5 5
-3 | 2
```

Figure 4.1

The range of the residuals is 54. The machine effects are reproduced in the table below.

Machine	1	2	3	4
effect	−166.25	−38.75	+38.75	+166.25

Since the difference between any pair of machines is greater than 54, it seems that the four sewing machines really differ in the speeds at which they may be used, with machine 4 the fastest and machine 1 the slowest.

With a Latin square design you can compare several different treatments when the experimental units fall into blocks under two different criteria. In the hemming example, the four sewing machines are the treatments, and their rate of operation is the response variable. The rate of operation of the machines is expected to depend on both the fabric type and the operator of the machine (these are the two blocking criteria).

Using sweeping by means to analyse Latin squares means you are trying to fit an additive (linear) model to the data. If there is a pattern in the residuals, this suggests as usual that the additive model is not appropriate. If the additive model is appropriate, and the treatment effects are larger than the residuals, you can reasonably conclude that there is a real difference between the treatments.

Exercise 4A

1. The Latin square and the numbers of items hemmed in one day in another hemming experiment are shown in the table below.

Operator

	A	B	C	D
P	900	1020	1150	1290
Q	1210	930	1060	1200
R	1150	1270	1000	1140
S	1040	1160	1290	1030

Fabric type (rows P, Q, R, S)

Operator

	A	B	C	D
P	1	2	3	4
Q	4	1	2	3
R	3	4	1	2
S	2	3	4	1

Fabric type (rows P, Q, R, S)

Which type of machine should be purchased?

2. An experiment to compare the effects on the milk yield of 4 different diets fed to cows during the winter uses a Latin square design. The diets are referred to as A, B, C and D, and the cows are referred to as P, Q R and S. The diets were allocated to the cows as shown in the Latin square below, over 4 different three-week periods referred to as 1, 2, 3 and 4. Each cow was fed the appropriate diet for the full three weeks, and the milk yield in litres was recorded in the final week. (The yields in the first two weeks were not recorded as part of the experimental data because they might include some carry-over effects from the previous diet. The details of the

experimental design and the milk yields are given below. (Table entries show diet followed by milk yield in litres.)

Cow

		P	Q	R	S
Period	1	A: 109	B: 111	C: 166	D: 141
	2	B: 108	D: 115	A: 124	C: 119
	3	C: 122	A: 79	D: 139	B: 93
	4	D: 126	C: 86	B: 116	A: 76

Analyse these results and report on them.

3. Three different timings of application of a top dressing of nitrogen fertiliser are to be compared in their effects on the yields of three varieties of wheat. Three fields are available and so a Latin square design is used. The patterns of application and the resulting yields in kg ha⁻¹ are shown in the table.

Variety of Wheat

		Haven	Hereward	Riband
Field	1	Y: 7400	Z: 7900	X: 7500
	2	X: 8100	Y: 7900	Z: 7300
	3	Z: 7300	X: 7600	Y: 7700

(i) Are you able to reach any firm conclusion concerning the effectiveness of the different timing patterns for applying the fertiliser?
(ii) Do your conclusions depend upon the variety of wheat being grown?
(iii) Do any patterns of application appear to be especially effective for any particular variety/varieties?

Factorial designs

A chemical company wishes to investigate the effects of the reaction temperature, the concentration, and the type of catalyst used, on the yield of a particular chemical process. A pilot plant has been constructed to run under various conditions, so that each of these variables can be set at one of two values as follows.

Variable	Possible values
Temperatures	150°C or 170°C
Concentrations	20% or 35%
Catalyst	X or Y.

How should the experiment be designed?

Except in the case of the Latin squares, which had their own special restrictions, the situations you have met so far have all consisted of experimental material, possibly in blocks, to which several treatments (or factors) are applied. In each case, however, each experimental unit received only one treatment.

The situation here is different: it is necessary to try the variables in various combinations. A factorial design can be used. The various treatments are called the *factors* and the different possibilities for these are called the *levels*. In this example, the factors are the temperature, the concentration and the catalyst. For each of these factors there are only two levels (choices) - called *high* or *low*. In some cases there might be more than two levels for each factor. For example, the company might wish to consider an intermediate temperature too. However, in many cases it is sufficient to consider just two possibilities. In a pilot experiment it is usual to limit the number of levels to the two extreme values of each factor.

There are eight (2x2x2) possibilities in total, ranging from setting all three factors at low level, to setting them all at high level. One possible notation is to represent the low level of the first factor by a and the high level by A, and so on.

If there were only 2 factors, the possible combinations would be

$$ab \quad Ab \quad aB \quad AB.$$

In the 2 factor case, it is helpful to represent the 4 possibilities as the vertices of a square (figure 4.2).

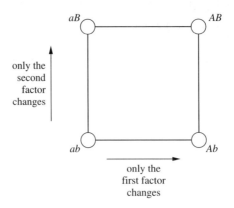

Figure 4.2

In the chemical plant example, which has 3 factors, the possible combinations are

$$abc \quad Abc \quad aBc \quad abC \quad ABc \quad AbC \quad aBC \quad ABC.$$

These 8 ($2 \times 2 \times 2$) possibilities can be represented as the vertices of a cube (figure 4.3).

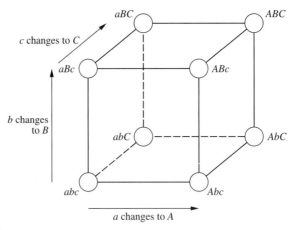

Figure 4.3

If there were 4 factors, the number of possible combinations would be

$$2 \times 2 \times 2 \times 2 = 16.$$

In this case you would need 4 dimensions to represent the possible combinations of the factors diagrammatically. For an experiment with n factors, each of which could be at one of two levels, there would be 2^n possible combinations, ranging from every factor being at the 'low' level, to every factor being at the 'high' level. For this reason, such experiments are often referred to as 2^n *factorial experiments*.

Analysis of data from factorial experiments

In a situation with n factors, you could think of these 2^n different combinations as 2^n separate treatments and look at the effect of each one. However, you will see that it is possible to obtain much more information by exploiting the fact that all possible combinations are present.

For example, consider the case of only three factors. As listed above, the possible combinations are:

$$abc \quad Abc \quad aBc \quad abC \quad ABc \quad AbC \quad aBC \quad ABC$$

Suppose you wish to look at the effect of having a high or a low level of the first factor. The combinations involving a low level of the first factor are

$$abc \quad aBc \quad abC \quad aBC.$$

You can see that in figure 4.3 these are all on the left face of the cube.

Those involving a high level of the first factor are

$$Abc \quad ABc \quad AbC \quad ABC.$$

These are all on the right face of the cube. You can see that we have actually compared the effect of the first factor in 4 different situations: we have compared a and A when combined with bc, Bc, bC and BC. The corresponding experiments are linked by horizontal lines. You can think of this as a paired design for a and A with 4 blocks defined by bc, bC, Bc and BC.

For each experiment there will usually be a numerical value for the response variable. In the chemical pilot plant this is the yield of the desired product. Using aBC (in ordinary type rather than italics) to represent the value of the response variable when the factors are at these levels, the effect of A over a is given by the values of Abc – abc, ABc – aBc, AbC – abC and ABC – aBC.

If the first treatment has no effect on the response variable, these four values should all be near to zero. The further they are away from zero, the greater is the apparent effect of the first treatment.

To estimate the mean effect of A over a you calculate the mean of these differences:

$$\tfrac{1}{4}[(Abc - abc) + (ABc - aBc) + (AbC - abC) + (ABC - aBC)]$$

Similarly, to compare the effect of B over b you use:

$$\tfrac{1}{4}[(aBc - abc) + (ABc - Abc) + (aBC - abC) + (ABC - AbC)]$$

Expressions like these are called *contrasts*, because they contrast the effects of the two levels of a factor.

Activity

Write down the contrast used to compare the effect of *C* over *c*, i.e. catalyst X and catalyst Y. If catalyst X were better than catalyst Y, would you expect your contrast to be positive or negative?

The results of the initial set of pilot plant trials are given in the table and in figure 4.4.

Temperature:	a (150 °C)	or A (170°C)	a	A	a	a	a	A	A	A
Concentration:	b (20%)	or B (35%)	b	b	B	b	B	b	B	B
Catalyst:	c (X)	or C (Y)	c	c	c	C	C	C	c	C
Yield in grams			59	74	50	50	46	81	69	79

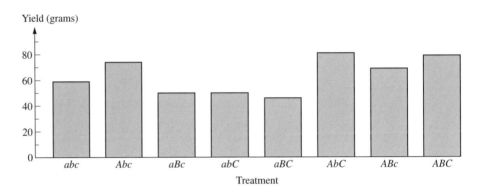

Figure 4.4   Plot of yield in grams against the treatment

Alternatively, the yields may be shown on the cube as in figure 4.5.

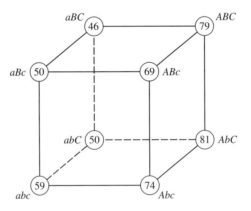

Figure 4.5

The mean effect of A over a is given by

$$\tfrac{1}{4}[(Abc - abc) + (ABc - aBc) + (AbC - abC) + (ABC - aBC)]$$
$$= \tfrac{1}{4}[(74 - 59) + (69 - 50) + (81 - 50) + (79 - 46)]$$
$$= \tfrac{1}{4}[15 + 19 + 31 + 33]$$
$$= \tfrac{98}{4}$$
$$= 24.5.$$

Activity

For the data above calculate the mean effects of B over b and C over c. Which treatment has the greatest effect on the yield?

For Discussion

In many cases, companies have felt that it was not necessary to spend the time and money involved in factorial experiments. They have argued that it is only necessary to conduct the experiment with all of the factors at the low level and then one experiment with each factor at a high level and the others at a low level. (This is sometimes referred to as the *one factor at a time* approach.) In the case of three factors this would mean performing experiments with the levels as *abc, Abc, aBc,* and *abC.* This would halve the number of experiments. (The approach gives even greater savings if there are more than three factors.)

The argument is that the other experiments are unnecessary because the effect of *ABc* could be found just by adding the effects of *Abc* and *aBc.* What assumption is being made?

Do the data in the chemical plant example suggest that the assumption is valid in this case?

NOTE *If you are sure that you do not need all of the information supplied by the full factorial approach, it is sometimes possible to reduce the number of experiments. One method of doing this is called the* Taguchi method, *after the man who developed it: it has been widely used in recent years, despite receiving quite a lot of criticism.*

Interactions

Returning to the general case, consider again the four contrasts of the effect of the first treatment:

$$Abc - abc, \quad ABc - aBc, \quad AbC - abC, \quad ABC - aBC.$$

If the effect of the treatments is additive, in other words if they are completely separate and do not affect each other, you would expect all of these values to be similar. Each one represents the difference in yield achieved by changing from a to A, whilst keeping the other treatment levels unchanged.

The assumption of additivity is not always valid: if two treatments are doing essentially the same thing their combined effect may not be much greater than the effect of one of them. For example, if you were testing two additives intended to strengthen a glue, they may have very similar effects when used individually, but combining the two treatments might have no greater result. On the other hand, it may be that neither of the treatments has an effect on its own, but that one is really a catalyst for the other. In this case, the effect of the two treatments used together would be much more than the effect of either of them used separately.

One way of identifying *interactions* between factors is to use a graph like those in figure 4.6.

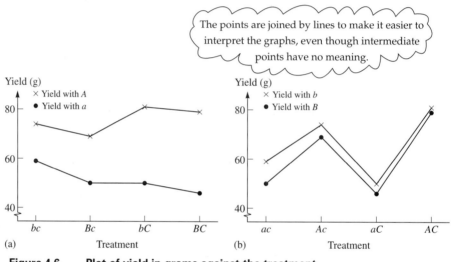

Figure 4.6   Plot of yield in grams against the treatment

If the effects were purely additive, that is if the treatments did not interact, the lines on the graphs would be parallel. The lines in (b) are nearly parallel, but those in (a) are not. On this basis, the effect of *b* over *B* seems to remain fairly constant, at about 7 g, (allowing for experimental variability). On the other hand, the effect of *A* over *a* seems to be greater when it is combined with *C* rather than *c*.

Another way of identifying and also quantifying interactions between the first factor and the second is to pair the comparisons for the first factor in a certain way. The approach is as follows.

In two of the comparisons, Abc − abc   and   AbC − abC, the second factor is at low level (*b*).

In the other two, ABc − aBc   and   ABC − aBC, the second factor is at high level (*B*).

If there is no interaction between the first two factors, then the expressions

$$\tfrac{1}{2}[(Abc - abc) + (AbC - abC)] \quad \text{and} \quad \tfrac{1}{2}[(ABc - aBc) + (ABC - aBC)]$$

both measure the mean effect of the first treatment, because the results have been paired in such a way that other effects should cancel each other out. They should have similar values.

However, if there is some interaction between A and B then the two expressions will not have similar values.

The difference between the two expressions,

$$\frac{(Abc - abc) + (AbC - abC)}{2} - \frac{(ABc - aBc) + (ABC - aBC)}{2}$$

gives some indication of whether there is an interaction between the first and second treatments.

The data for the chemical pilot experiment are given again in the table below.

			a	A	a	a	a	A	A	A
Temperature:	a (150 °C) or A (170°C)		a	A	a	a	a	A	A	A
Concentration:	b (20%) or B (35%)		b	b	B	b	B	b	B	B
Catalyst:	c (X) or C (Y)		c	c	c	C	C	C	c	C
Yield in grams			59	74	50	50	46	81	69	79

The interaction between the first and second treatments is given by

$$\frac{(Abc - abc) + (AbC - abC)}{2} + \frac{(ABc - aBc) + (ABC - aBC)}{2}$$

$$= \tfrac{1}{2}[(74 - 59) + (81 - 50) + (69 - 50) - (79 - 46)]$$

$$= -\tfrac{6}{2}$$

$$= -3$$

We have already found that the mean effect of A over a is 24.5 and the mean effect of B over b is about 7. Compared with these the interaction between the first and second factors is relatively small, and so we may probably ignore it. If the interaction effects had been large compared with the effects of the factors themselves, we should have been very wary of simply quoting the mean effects of the factors separately.

As for other experimental designs, randomisation is important. If the chemical plant is effectively in continuous operation, it will be the order of the different treatment allocations (abc, AbC, etc.) that will be randomised.

If the three factors in a 2^3 factorial experiment are more-or-less additive, then the effects of a and A are compared in four experiments and this provides a kind of replication. However, it is realistic to suppose that there will be some interactions, and so it is much better to provide replications by repeating the whole set of 8 experiments. If you want 5 replicates of each experiment, it will be necessary to perfom $5 \times 8 = 40$ experiments. The number of replications required will, of course, depend on the precision required, the resources available, and the time and cost implications of the experiments.

Exercise 4B

1. In agriculture, plants need Nitrogen, Phosphate and Potassium (often referred to as the NPK trio, because of their chemical symbols). The various fertilisers which are available contain different proportions of these three elements, as well as other important 'trace elements'.

   Describe a 2^3 factorial experiment to compare the effects of high and low proportions of these chemicals in a fertiliser on the yield of a crop of cabbages. Identify the factors, levels, experimental material, experimental units and the response variable.

2. In a second run of the pilot chemical plant, the following results were obtained.

Temperature: a (150°C) or A (170°C)	a A a a a A A A
Concentration: b (20%) or B (35%)	b b B b B b B B
Catalyst: c (X) or C (Y)	c c c C C C c C
Yield in grams	61 70 58 54 44 85 67 81

   Use these data to estimate the mean effects of the treatments and the interactions.

3. In a polymerisation plant, there is concern about the colour of the polymer being produced. The factors involved were as follows.
   - the concentration of the catalyst: 1% or 1.7%
   - the temperature of the reactor: 135°C or 185°C
   - the amount of additive: 1 kg or 6 kg

Run number	1	2	3	4	5	6	7	8
Concentration	1.7	1	1.7	1	1.7	1.7	1	1
Temperature	185	185	135	185	135	185	135	135
Additive	6	1	6	6	1	1	6	1
Colour	72	48	37	48	36	74	62	61

Find the mean effect of each of the three factors and investigate interactions between them. (High values for the colour correspond to a better result.)

4. A firm whose computers are too slow for the increasingly complex database work required of them is considering upgrading its current machines. There are three options:
   - replace the processors
   - increase the RAM
   - replace the hard disks.

   As well as testing the individual effects of these changes, the company wishes to know the effect of combining any two, or all three of them.

   How should the experiment be designed?

5. In the manufacture of a polymer used to make clear film for a wide variety of purposes, several factors are believed to affect the quality of the end product and the speed of the process.
   (i) The first factor to be considered is the addition of a catalyst, at several different levels, which it is hoped will decrease the polymerisation time. The current batch time is about 125 minutes. It was decided to use 2 replicates of the catalyst at 4 different levels. The results are shown in the table below.

Level of catalyst in ppm	Time 1 (minutes)	Time 2 (minutes)
50	125	123
100	102	109
200	94	96
300	90	95

   Plot the values on a graph and comment on the effect of the catalyst on the time for polymerisation.
   (ii) There are problems in using high levels of the catalyst as this tends to degrade the colour. It is believed that a stabiliser might reduce this effect.

Commercial and industrial statistics

Temperature is also believed to be a relevant factor and so a factorial experiment is conducted, with each factor at 2 levels. The results are given in the table below. In each case the colour was acceptable. What are your recommendations?

Catalyst (ppm)	Stabiliser (ppm)	Temperature (°C)	Polymerisation time (minutes)
150	50	280	125
150	50	300	94
150	100	280	129
150	100	300	97
250	50	280	112
250	50	300	75
250	100	280	118
250	100	300	86

(iii) The experimenter also ran two experiments at the intermediate levels, obtaining the results which are given in the following table. Do these extra values shed any further light (or doubt) on your conclusions?

Catalyst (ppm)	Stabiliser (ppm)	Temperature (°C)	Polymerisation time (minutes)
200	75	290	109
200	75	290	99

KEY POINTS

When you have worked through this chapter you should
- understand when a Latin square experimental design is useful
- be able to set up an experiment using a Latin square design
- be able to use the technique of sweeping by means to analyse a Latin square
- understand when a factorial experimental design is useful
- understand the terms *level, contrast* and *interaction* in the context of factorial experiments
- be able to analyse the results of factorial experiments and to identify any interactions between the factors.

Statistical quality control

A conjurer may pull a rabbit out of a hat, but he cannot pull quality out of a hat.

Dr William Edwards Deming

A car manufacturer is concerned by the increasing number of complaints from purchasers of its latest model. The complains are usually about minor faults that are quickly and easily corrected, but the faults are eroding customer confidence and loyalty.
- **With a limited budget, how can the manufacturer prioritise the work needed to reduce the number of complaints?**
- **What is the optimum method of checking the quality of components supplied to the manufacturer?**
- **What inspection procedures can be used during the production process to guarantee the quality of the finished product?**

Before the Second World War, Japanese goods were not highly regarded. Since that time the Japanese have taken quality control very seriously, and their products are now respected for their quality and reliability. The statistical techniques covered in this chapter and the next have been crucial in this transformation.

Although many of the methods were first developed in Europe and America (and indeed it was an American, Dr W.E. Deming, who introduced and popularised the methods in Japan), it was not until the early 1980s that companies in the USA implemented the same methods. European companies followed later. The methodology has developed further over the years, and is now seen as part of a broader framework generally referred to as *Total Quality Management (TQM)*.

Quality

A working definition of 'quality' would be 'fitness for purpose'. We expect a high quality product to do its job better than a low quality one. It also usually costs more to produce and to buy.

A high quality product must be well designed: its *quality of design* must be high. It must also be well made: it must have high *quality of conformance* to the design specification.

To achieve high quality of conformance, the manufacturer must ensure that
- the materials used are reliably good
- the machinery used is of sufficiently high precision and reliability
- the workforce is well trained and motivated.

Since none of these can ever be 100% guaranteed, it is necessary to keep a check on them. The techniques in these chapters help manufacturers to identify faults, and to locate their source. Remedial action can then be taken as quickly as possible. In some cases it is possible to identify when something is going wrong before faulty goods are produced.

Manufacturers are naturally concerned about the 'bottom line', the cost of production. Clearly, inspections during and after production will have a cost. However, the production of faulty goods will cost the company money in
- lost orders
- scrapped products
- reworked products
- lower selling price.

Thus it may be that inspection can reduce overall costs as well as improving the quality of the final product.

Pareto charts

The car manufacturer mentioned at the start of the chapter wants to ensure that customers are fully satisfied, and not inconvenienced by minor faults on their new cars. To achieve this a checklist is provided for car dealers to work through prior to handing over the car to the customer. The dealers are asked to keep a tally of items from the checklist that have required attention. During the first three months, 947 cars have been sold and the tally chart data have been summarised in the table below.

Item to be checked	Number of faults	Item to be checked	Number of faults
Front windscreen clean?	12	Boot light working?	8
Rear windscreen clean?	29	Horn working?	1
Windows clean?	52	Seats clean?	2
Front windscreen washer bottle full?	137	Headlights working?	0
		Headlights correctly adjusted?	0
Rear windscreen washer bottle full?	162	Rear lights working?	2
Radiator coolant level correct?	31	Radio working?	0
Oil level correct?	4	Trims fitted correctly?	1
All doors close correctly?	7	Bodywork free of blemishes?	2
Boot closes correctly?	11	Bodywork clean and polished?	27
Interior light working?	3	Manual in glove compartment?	164

The company is concerned about the number of items on the checklist that are requiring the dealers' attention, since everything should have been done at an earlier stage. How can this problem be addressed?

There is no point in just telling everyone on the production line that they need to be more diligent. The approach needs to be much more focused, and priorities identified.

A sensible approach is to try to deal with the most frequently-occurring faults first. It is helpful, therefore, to reorder the above list so that the items with the highest frequencies are at the top of the list. In order to make the situation clear, the faults and their frequencies are displayed on a bar chart (figure 5.1).

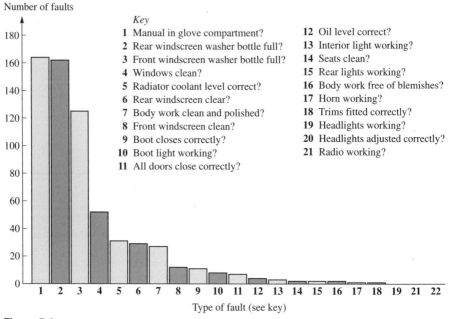

Number of faults

Key
1 Manual in glove compartment?
2 Rear windscreen washer bottle full?
3 Front windscreen washer bottle full?
4 Windows clean?
5 Radiator coolant level correct?
6 Rear windscreen clear?
7 Body work clean and polished?
8 Front windscreen clean?
9 Boot closes correctly?
10 Boot light working?
11 All doors close correctly?

12 Oil level correct?
13 Interior light working?
14 Seats clean?
15 Rear lights working?
16 Body work free of blemishes?
17 Horn working?
18 Trims fitted correctly?
19 Headlights working?
20 Headlights adjusted correctly?
21 Radio working?

Type of fault (see key)

Figure 5.1

The bar chart shows very clearly which items are causing the most problems, and how frequently these problems occur compared with the others on the list. To tackle the most frequent faults, changes may be needed in the way things are done at the factory or at the garage. The chart doesn't solve the problem, it is simply a tool which helps to identify the problem.

The car manufacturer still needs to decide how many of the items can be dealt with initially. A simple empirical rule, which has been found to be satisfactory in most circumstances, is to deal with those items which cause 80% of the faults. You could find this from the sorted list but it is helpful to use a cumulative frequency chart (as in figure 5.2).

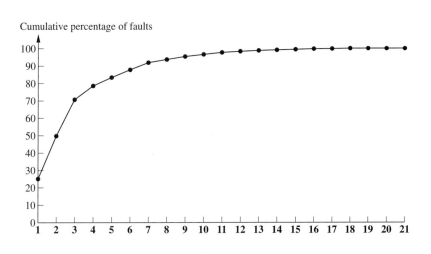

Cumulative percentage of faults

Figure 5.2

The bar chart and the cumulative frequency chart are called *Pareto charts* (after an Italian economist who believed that about 90% of the wealth of his country was owned by about 10% of the population). They help people to focus on the main problems and not just the obvious ones: you can see that about 80% of the defects can be eliminated by addressing just 20% of the possible causes. The empirical *80–20 rule* also provides a cut off point for how far down the list to go in the first instance.

For Discussion

On which of the faults in the checklist should the car manufacturer concentrate in order to eliminate 80% of the defects in the cars?

After action had been taken on the points identified by the Pareto analysis, there would usually be further inspections. These would
* check that the action had been effective, i.e. the number of faults in the areas picked out by the first analysis had been dramatically reduced, and
* highlight the areas requiring attention next.

The analysis above concentrated on the **number** of faults that occurred in the cars. In other circumstances, it may be appropriate to focus instead on the **cost of remedying** the faults. In a factory, the production-line workers would tend to be concerned about the number of faults, whereas the management might be more concerned about the associated costs. In this kind of situation, a Pareto analysis would probably be carried out on both features.

Pareto chart analysis is usually used in situations where all of the products are inspected – 100% inspection. The company policy may be that non-conforming products are scrapped, repaired, or sold at a lower price. All of these cost the company money and so it is important to reduce or eliminate the faults if possible. By using Pareto charts, effort can be concentrated in the most sensible way, rather than on the most obvious problems.

1. A firm manufacturing textiles monitors the quality of the batches of yarn that it produces.

Reason for rejection	Number of occurrences
Weight incorrect	82
Blend incorrect	70
Uneven	43
Thick place fault	25
Thin place fault	22
Dirty	13
Incomplete	7
Damaged (miscellaneous)	2

Perform a Pareto analysis on the data and report on which faults should be dealt with first.

2. A company manufacturing parts for fork-lift trucks is concerned about the number of faulty parts produced during the last month. You are asked to analyse the data and to produce some recommendations for improving the situation. The faults are listed according to the machine which produced the part. Use a Pareto analysis to identify which machines will need attention if the number of faulty parts is to be reduced by 80%.

Machine/Process	Number of faulty parts
Horizontal machining centre	5
Vertical machining centre	45
Special purpose milling machine	10
Robot-fed lathe A	46
Robot-fed lathe B	11
Robot-fed lathe C	70
Heavy duty lathe	7
Heavy duty shaft-turning lathe	19
Bar-fed lathe	9
Chucking lathe	4
Special purpose drill	4
Unspecified	2

3. The quality assurance manager of a firm that manufactures carriage clocks notes that a variety of faults can lead to rejection of the finished clocks. The people who are making the final check of the completed clocks are asked to record the reasons for rejecting clocks over a period of one month. The results of this, and the cost of repairing each type of fault, are given in the table.

Fault code	Description	Number of rejects	Cost of repair (£)
A	timing mechanism	7	3
B	marks on clock face	194	1
C	clock face not fitting properly	11	2
D	pointers not fitting correctly	10	1
E	the pointers being marked or bent	89	1
F	marks on the casing	17	2
G	the casing not fitting the mechanism properly	3	3
H	the handle being badly made	1	1
I	the handle not being fitted correctly to the casing	0	1
J	the door hinges not operating correctly	2	1
K	the door fastener not working	1	1
TOTAL		335	–

(i) Use Pareto charts to analyse the number of faults of each type, and summarise your findings in a brief report.

(ii) Produce a second Pareto analysis based on the cost of repairing the different types of fault.

(iii) Taking both analyses into account, on which faults would you suggest the company focuses more of its attention in the immediate future?

4. A firm producing parts for the automotive industry is trying to reduce the number that are rejected at the final inspection. You have been asked to recommend which parts of the manufacturing process should be targeted in order to bring about the greatest decrease in the number of rejects. The number of rejects for last month and the machine/process with which they are associated are given in the table, together with the cost of reworking or remaking each part.

Perform two Pareto analyses: one based on the number of rejects from each machine and one based on the cost of correcting the situation. What are your recommendations?

Machine/ Process	Number of rejects	Cost of repair/ rework (£)
Pillar drill	7	10
Bench drill	2	8
Precision drill	5	12
Flatbed lathe A	23	5
Flatbed lathe B	16	5
Flatbed lathe C	35	5
Special boring machine 1	20	20
Special boring machine 2	3	20
Automatic rotary welding machine	22	6
Hydraulic welding machine	8	3
Unspecified	2	–

Acceptance sampling

Many companies process items or materials that have been produced by someone else. For example, computer firms often buy in components to assemble computers, then sell the finished product, usually to a retailer. The philosophy of *Total Quality Management* involves seeing one part of the firm as the supplier for another part, so that each stage in production has to achieve clearly defined quality objectives.

In many situations it is neither economic nor feasible to check every item coming into a factory. A 100% inspection scheme would generally be far too expensive in time and money. In fact, experience shows that 100% inspection only finds about 80% of the faults, since the work is monotonous and inspectors find it hard to maintain their concentration. Another consideration is that in cases where testing an item renders it unsuitable for use, 100% inspection would mean that there would be no items left to process! *Testing to destruction* is important in some fields: it is used to test the strength of badminton racquet handles, the taste of food products and the life-time of a light bulb.

An alternative to 100% inspection is to take a sample from a batch of items, and to use the quality of the sample as an indicator of the quality of the batch. If there are too many faulty items in the sample, the whole batch is rejected. The testing is usually done by the purchaser before accepting the items. A *batch* might be a crate of components, a tanker of chemical or a bale of cotton. The firm receiving the batch would like it to be homogenous, so that a sample should be representative of the whole batch. If the supplier provides good documentation with each batch, any likely variations can be identified. A supplier of cloth for a clothes manufacturer might for example point out that a certain lorry-load contains cloth made from yarn from two different sources. The clothes manufacturer can then test a sample from each of these strata.

Acceptance sampling can only be used where there are clearly defined conformance criteria: the item either conforms to the specification or it doesn't. A tennis ball might be tested by dropping it from a height of 1.5 m and then checking whether the height of its bounce is in a required range. A porcelain vase would need a rather different test! It might be assessed subjectively by an inspector as being suitable or not suitable for sale. In cases where the assessment is subjective, it is usual to provide examples of items which are clearly satisfactory, just satisfactory, just unsatisfactory and clearly unsatisfactory: this ensures that the inspector knows what is acceptable. If there are several inspectors it is sensible to compare their decisions, to make sure that all are equally strict.

The first step in setting up an acceptance sampling scheme is to decide on the maximum proportion of non-conforming items that is acceptable in a batch. This proportion is called p_0. The aim of the scheme is to check that the proportion of non-conforming items in a batch does not exceed p_0.

In a *single sampling* scheme, the decision to accept or reject the batch is made on the basis of a single random sample from the batch. In a *double sampling* scheme, a second random sample is taken if the first sample does not give a sufficiently clear indication of the quality of the batch.

Whichever type of scheme is used, it is always possible that the sample is not representative of the batch. The aim is to accept batches in which the proportion of non-conforming items is less than or equal to p_0, and to reject batches in which the proportion of non-conforming items is greater than p_0. The ideal scheme is summarised in figure 5.3(a). You can never guarantee this without 100% inspection, but by looking at the corresponding graph for any sampling scheme you can see how close it is to the ideal.

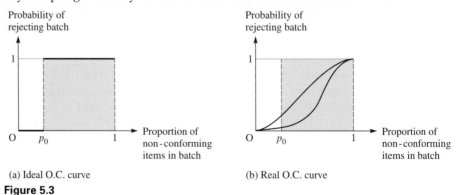

(a) Ideal O.C. curve

(b) Real O.C. curve

Figure 5.3

A graph showing the probability of rejecting the batch against the proportion of defects, as in figure 5.3, is called the *operating characteristic curve* of the sampling scheme.

NOTE *Some people define the operating characteristic curve as the graph of the probability of **accepting** the batch against the proportion of non-conforming items.*

For Discussion

Which of the two curves in figure 5.3(b) represents a better sampling procedure? Explain your answer in terms of the likelihood of rejecting an acceptable batch and of accepting an unacceptable batch.

Since samples are not always representative, batches which should have been accepted will sometimes be rejected, and batches which should have been rejected will sometimes be accepted.

- The probability of rejecting a batch which should have been accepted is often referred to as the *producer's risk*.
- The probability of accepting a batch which should have been rejected is often referred to as the *consumer's risk*.

The possibilities are summarised in the table.

		Actual condition	
		Batch acceptable	Batch not acceptable
Decision based on sample	Batch accepted	Correct decision	Incorrect decision
	Batch rejected	Incorrect decision	Correct decision

The situation is equivalent to the standard hypothesis-testing framework. If the maximum allowable proportion of non-conforming items in the batch is p_0, and the actual (unknown) proportion is p then you have the following hypotheses:

Null Hypothesis (NH): $p \le p_0$

Alternative Hypothesis (AH): $p > p_0$.

Using the standard hypothesis-testing terms, the table is now as shown below.

		Actual condition	
		NH True	NH False
Decision based on sample	Accept NH	Correct decision	Type I error (consumer's risk)
	Reject NH	Type I error (producer's risk)	Correct decision

To calculate the probabilities of rejecting batches for different proportions of non-conforming items, you need to model the sampling schemes. You can then compare different sampling schemes to see which will work best in a particular situation.

Commercial and industrial statistics

Single sampling schemes

A company that assembles televisions purchases the tubes from a supplier in batches of 200. To check the quality of the tubes that it receives, the company checks 10 tubes from each batch before deciding whether to accept the batch. The company is willing to accept a maximum of 2% faulty tubes in any batch (i.e. not more than 4 in batch of 200). Imposing a stricter demand would result in the supplier charging a higher price for the tubes (because extra inspection costs would be incurred by the supplier).

How many faulty tubes in a sample should result in the batch being rejected? Is this an effective sampling scheme? How good is it at detecting when more than 2% of the tubes in a batch are faulty?

Modelling the sampling scheme

If the true proportion of non-conforming items in the batch is p, and we take a random sample of size n from the batch, the number of non-conforming items in the sample, r, is modelled by the random variable R, where

$$R \sim B(n, p).$$

This assumes that the proportion of non-conforming items being produced is fairly constant during the production of the batch, and that the items are placed in the batch in a random way.

In a single sampling scheme, the decision to accept or reject the batch is made on the basis of one sample. Suppose that the *decision rule* is that the batch will be accepted if there are c or fewer non-conforming items, and it will be rejected if there are more than c non-conforming items (see figure 5.4).

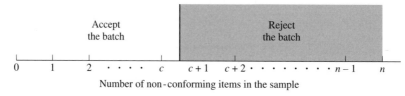

Accept the batch | Reject the batch

0 1 2 · · · · c $c+1$ $c+2$ · · · · · · · · $n-1$ n

Number of non-conforming items in the sample

Figure 5.4

The probability of rejecting the batch when the actual proportion of non-conforming items is p, is

$$P(R > c) = P(R = c+1) + P(R = c+2) + \ldots + P(R = n)$$
$$= {}^nC_{c+1}p^{c+1}(1-p)^{n-c-1} + {}^nC_{c+2}p^{c+2}(1-p)^{n-c-2} + \ldots + p^n.$$

On the other hand, the probability of accepting the batch when the proportion of non-conforming items is p is

$$P(R \le c) = P(R = 0) + P(R = 1) + \ldots + P(R = c)$$
$$= (1-p)^n + {}^nC_1 p(1-p)^{n-1} + \ldots + {}^nC_c p^c (1-p)^{n-c}.$$

Using these two results you can work out the proportion of batches that would be rejected for any value of p. You can do this for different values of c to find out which value gives the best results.

NOTE

A more accurate approach is to think of the sample of size n as coming from a batch of size N which actually contains x non-conforming items. The number of non-conforming items in the batch, r, actually comes from a hypergeometric *distribution. If you model the number of non-conforming items in the batch by the random variable, R, you see that*

$$P(R = r) = \frac{{}^{x}C_{r}\,{}^{N-x}C_{n-r}}{{}^{N}C_{n}} \text{ for } r = 0, 1, 2, \ldots, min(x, n),$$

since you are taking r non-conforming items from a total of x non-conforming items in the batch, and therefore (n − r) conforming items from the (N − x) conforming items in the batch.

If the sample size is fairly small compared to the batch size, the binomial distribution is a satisfactory approximation to the hypergeometric distribution. This is true for all of the examples in this book.

Going back now to the company assembling televisions, there are two decisions to make about the sampling scheme: how large a sample should be taken from each batch of tubes, and where do you draw the line for accepting a batch? What value of c gives the best results?

The answers to these questions depend of course on:
- What proportion of non-conforming items you are prepared to accept in the batch
- What proportion of non-conforming items you are not prepared to accept in the batch
- How much time and money you are willing to spend on inspection.

For now, however, we shall focus mainly on the effects of altering the sample size and the decision rule, since these are the specifically statistical questions.

Suppose that the proportion of faulty tubes in a batch is 2%, and that you take a sample size of 10. The probabilities of finding various numbers of faulty tubes in the sample are given in the table below.

Number of faulty tubes in the sample of size 10	0	1	2	3 or more
Probability	0.8171	0.1667	0.0153	0.0009

The table shows that in this situation you would not be surprised to find zero or 1 faulty tubes in a sample of size 10. The probability of finding 2 or more is 0.0162 or 1.62%. So a reasonable rule would be to reject the batch if 2 or more faulty tubes were found in a sample of size 10. With this rule ($c = 1$), the probabilities of rejecting a batch for various values of p are given in the next table.

p	0.01	0.02	0.03	0.04	0.05	0.06	0.07	0.08	0.09	0.10
P(reject)	0.0043	0.0162	0.0345	0.0582	0.0861	0.1176	0.1517	0.1879	0.225	0.2639

What would be the effect in the same situation of using samples of size 15 instead of 10? Would the extra cost be worthwhile?

To work this out, you need to know the probabilities of finding various numbers of faulty tubes in a sample of size 15 when the proportion in the batch is 2%. These probabilities are given in the table below.

Number of faulty tubes in the sample of size 15	0	1	2	3 or more
Probability	0.7386	0.2261	0.0323	0.0030

The table suggests that you would not be surprised to find zero or 1 faulty tubes in a sample of size 15. The probability of finding 2 or more in the sample is 0.0353 or 3.53%. So, in this situation too, a reasonable rule would be to reject the batch if 2 or more faulty tubes were found in the sample. With this rule ($c = 1$), the probabilities of rejecting a batch for various values of p are given below.

p	0.01	0.02	0.03	0.04	0.05	0.06	0.07	0.08	0.09	0.10
P(reject)	0.0096	0.0353	0.0730	0.1191	0.1710	0.2262	0.2832	0.3403	0.3965	0.4510

The operating characteristic curves for the two sample sizes are shown in figure 5.5.

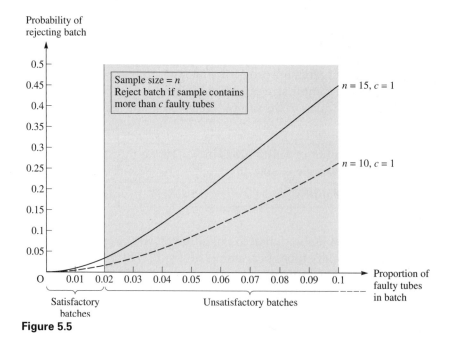

Figure 5.5

Commercial and industrial statistics

From the graphs you can see that whatever the proportion of faulty tubes in the batch, using a sample size of 15 makes you almost twice as likely to reject a batch as when you are using a sample size of 10. If the proportion of faulty tubes in the batches is too high, this will be an advantage. It will be a disadvantage, though, if the proportion of faulty tubes is within the required range.

What happens if you use a sample size of 15, but take $c = 2$? This means that you reject a batch if the sample contains more than 2 faulty tubes. The operating characteristic curve is shown in figure 5.6.

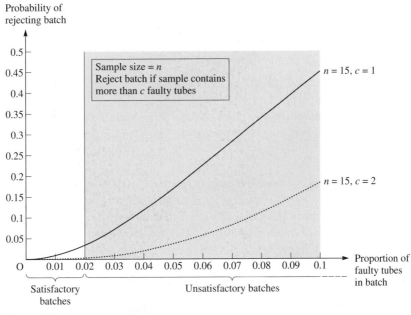

Figure 5.6

With samples of size 15 you are much less likely to reject a batch using $c = 2$ than using $c = 1$. This means that you will reject fewer satisfactory batches. However, using $n = 15$ and $c = 2$ means that you will also accept many more unsatisfactory batches.

What happens if you use a sample of size 20 with $c = 2$? Under this scheme you reject batches with 3 or more faulty tubes. The OC curves for this and the other three schemes that have been considered are shown in figure 5.7.

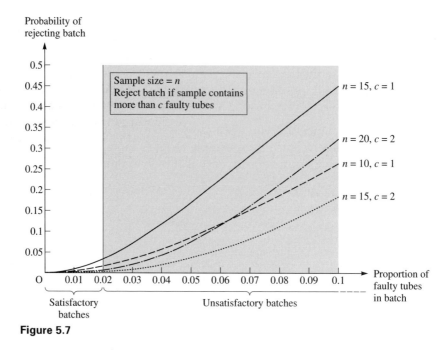

Figure 5.7

You can now see the advantage of using a sample of size 20. The probability of rejecting the batch is kept small while the proportion of faulty tubes is satisfactory (less than 2%), but increases quite quickly once the proportion of faulty tubes becomes unsatisfactory. However, taking a larger sample will usually increase the cost of the scheme in both time and money. If the tubes have to be tested to destruction, the costs are even higher: many acceptable tubes will be lost in the testing process.

The table below can be helpful when deciding which inspection scheme to use. The possible outcomes are similar to those which occur in a hypothesis testing situation. Sometimes it is helpful to put relative weights, or even financial values, on the different outcomes.

	Batch satisfactory	Batch unsatisfactory
Accept batch	✔	Customer Complaints
Reject Batch	Wasted Products	✔

The final choice of sampling scheme may depend upon the reputation of the supplier of the tubes. If the supplier is new, or has recently supplied many unsatisfactory batches, it may be best to choose a sampling scheme that is more likely to reject batches. If the supplier has a good reputation it may be better to choose a scheme that is more likely to accept batches.

1. Which of the four sampling schemes described in the text would you use if the tube-supplier were new? Which would you use if the supplier had established a good reputation?

2. A large motor manufacturer buys some parts from other firms and expects very high quality. The sample size used in the inspection varies according to the recent reliability of the supplier. The decision rule is always that the only batches accepted are those with zero non-conforming items in the sample. The items come in very large batches.

   Draw the OC curves to show how effective the sampling scheme is in detecting proportions of non-conforming items up to 5% for sample sizes of 10, 20, 50 and 100.

3. An electronic thickness-measuring gauge is used to check the chrome plating on shafts which are delivered to a factory in batches of 500. The thickness of the plating should be 25±5 microns. The factory is willing to accept batches with up to 2% non-conforming items. The manager feels that the chrome plating on a random sample of 10% of the shafts in each batch, i.e. 50 shafts, should be checked. The production manager is concerned about the time involved in doing this and feels that a sample of 25 should be sufficient.

   Compare these two schemes for batches containing up to 5% non-conforming items. What scheme would you recommend?

4. A large DIY store buys substantial numbers of plants from a local market-garden. As the price is very competitive the manager is willing to allow up to 5% of the plants to be substandard. The plants are checked visually for growth above and below the soil. The manager specifies a random sampling scheme to check 50 of the plants from each batch (lorry load).

   What sampling scheme should be used if the manager wants the probability of rejecting a lorry load with 5% substandard to be 0.05 or less? Draw the OC curve for this scheme.

Double sampling schemes

Double sampling schemes overcome some of the problems associated with single sampling schemes. Instead of accepting or rejecting the batch on the basis of a single sample, a second sample can be taken to obtain further information when the result of the first sample is not conclusive. If the number of non-conforming items in the initial sample is very low, the batch will be accepted. If the number of non-conforming items in the initial sample is very high, the batch will be rejected. If neither of these applies, a second sample will be taken and the decision will be based on the information from both samples together.

The average number of items inspected in each batch under a double sampling scheme clearly lies somewhere between the number in the first sample and the total of the first and second sample. A double sampling scheme with n_1 items in the first sample and n_2 items in the second sample
- is more sensitive than a single sampling scheme with n_1 items, and
- inspects fewer items in the long run than a single sampling scheme with $(n_1 + n_2)$ items.

A double sampling scheme is more complex to design, and slightly more difficult to operate than a single sampling scheme. To see how double-sampling might work, we shall look again at the company receiving television tubes. As before, a batch with up to 2% of its tubes faulty is counted as satisfactory. The initial sample is of size 10. For a batch in which 2% or 10% of the tubes are faulty, the probabilities of the sample containing various numbers of faulty tubes are given in the table below.

Number of faulty tubes in a sample of 10	0	1	2	3 or more
Probability when 2% of tubes in batch are faulty	0.8171	0.1667	0.0153	0.0009
Probability when 10% of tubes in batch are faulty	0.3487	0.3874	0.1937	0.0702

You can see that it is highly unlikely that there will be 3 or more faulty tubes in a sample of 10 from a satisfactory batch: the probability is about 0.0009 (0.09%). If there are 3 or more faulty tubes in a sample, it is more likely that the batch contains too high a proportion of faulty tubes. This suggests that you should reject straight away any batch for which a sample of size 10 contains 3 or more faulty tubes.

If there are no faulty tubes in the sample of 10, the batch should certainly be accepted. Therefore, when the proportion of faulty tubes is 2%, the probability of our accepting a batch after sampling only 10 items is 0.8171. The remaining batches, those for which the sample contains 1 or 2 faulty tubes, would have a second sample taken. The scheme is summarised in the table below.

Number of faulty tubes in the first sample of size 10	Action to be taken	Probability of this when underlying proportion of faulty tubes is 2%
zero	accept the batch	0.8171
1 or 2	take a second sample	0.1820
3 or more	reject the batch	0.0009

The sampling scheme above would lead to almost a fifth of satisfactory batches (18.2%) having a second sample checked. Notice that even when the proportion of faulty tubes in each batch rises as high as 10%, about 35% of the batches will be accepted without further testing.

You are now left with batches for which the sample of 10 contains 1 or 2 faulty tubes. In these cases you require a second sample. Suppose you decide that the second sample should also be of size 10: this means that if there are 1 or 2 faulty tubes in the first sample, a second sample of 10 will be taken and so a total of 20 items will be inspected.

To decide when to accept or reject batches on the basis of a second sample, you need to know the probabilities of the various possible outcomes. Since the samples are independent, you multiply their probabilities. For example, the probability of there being 1 faulty tube in the first sample and 2 in the second sample is

$$P(R = 1)P(R = 2)$$

The table below gives the probabilities in which we are interested for a batch in which 2% of the tubes are faulty.

r	0	1	2	3 or more
Probability of 1 faulty tube in 1st sample and r in 2nd sample ($p = 0.02$)	0.1362	0.0278	0.0026	0.0002
Probability of 2 faulty tubes in 1st sample and r in 2nd sample ($p = 0.02$)	0.0125	0.0026	0.0002	0

Note that zero means in this case a probability of less than 0.000 05

You can see that it is highly unlikely that there will be 1 faulty tube in the first sample and then 2 or more in the second sample. The probability is only 0.0028. Similarly it is highly unlikely that there will be 2 faulty tubes in the first sample and 1 or more in the second sample. The probability is again 0.0028. So if there are 3 or more faulty tubes in the combined sample it is likely that the batch contains too high a proportion of faulty tubes. It should be rejected.

This sampling scheme is shown in the tree diagram in figure 5.8.

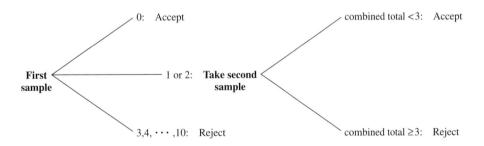

Figure 5.8

If the actual proportion of faulty tubes in the batch is p and the number of faulty tubes in a sample of size 10 is modelled by the random variable R, then $R{\sim}B(10, p)$ and

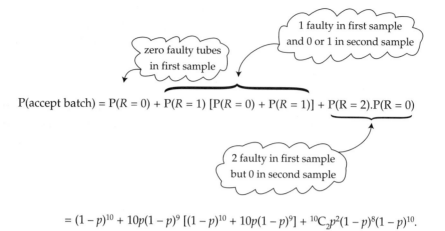

$$P(\text{accept batch}) = P(R = 0) + P(R = 1) [P(R = 0) + P(R = 1)] + P(R = 2).P(R = 0)$$

1 faulty in first sample and 0 or 1 in second sample

zero faulty tubes in first sample

2 faulty in first sample but 0 in second sample

$$= (1 - p)^{10} + 10p(1 - p)^9 [(1 - p)^{10} + 10p(1 - p)^9] + {}^{10}C_2 p^2 (1 - p)^8 (1 - p)^{10}.$$

The probability of rejecting a batch with various proportions of faulty tubes is given in the next table. Figure 5.9 presents the operating characteristic curve for this scheme together with those for single sampling schemes with sample sizes of 10 and 20.

p	0.01	0.02	0.03	0.04	0.05	0.06	0.07	0.08	0.09	0.10
P(reject)	0.001	0.006	0.019	0.040	0.069	0.105	0.147	0.195	0.246	0.299

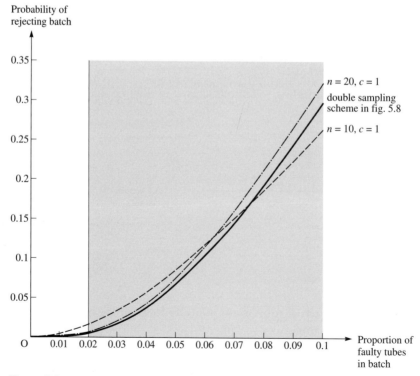

Figure 5.9

The OC curves give you a great deal of information. To decide which sampling scheme is most appropriate for the situation, you need to look at how they work when the number of faulty tubes is at an acceptable level and when there are too many faulty tubes.

Quality acceptable

When the proportion of faulty tubes is at the accepted level (0.02 or less), the single sampling scheme with $n = 10$ is about twice as likely to reject a batch as the other two schemes. Rejecting satisfactory batches is wasteful of time and money and causes friction with the supplier, so this scheme is undesirable. The double sampling scheme tests fewer items than the single sampling scheme with $n = 20$, so, the double sampling scheme is best during normal operation. This is the situation that should apply for most of the time once a supplier is established.

Quality unacceptable

When the proportion of faulty tubes is just above the accepted level, the single sampling scheme with $n = 10$ is the best, because it gives the highest probability of rejecting the batch. If the proportion of faulty tubes reaches 7%, the single sampling scheme with $n = 20$ is the best. If the proportion of faulty tubes reaches 15% or more, the double sampling scheme is the best.

Average number of items sampled

An important aspect of a sampling scheme is the average number of items that are actually examined, since this determines a large part of the cost of the scheme. Under the double sampling scheme when the percentage of faulty tubes is exactly 2%, the number of tubes examined is either 10 or 20. If there are 1 or 2 faulty tubes in the first sample, a second sample is taken.

The probability of this happening is

$$0.1667 + 0.0153 = 0.1820$$

probability of 1 faulty tube in first sample

probability of 2 faulty tubes in first sample

Therefore, when the percentage of faulty tubes is 2% the average number inspected is

$$20 \times 0.1820 + 10 \times 0.8180 = 11.82.$$

probability of no second sample

Under normal operation, the double sampling scheme requires far fewer tubes to be examined than the single sampling scheme with $n = 20$.

For Discussion

When a batch fails to meet the acceptance criterion it will probably be returned to the supplier. In some cases, of course, the supplier will be another section of the same firm. The supplier must make a decision as to what happens to rejected batches. They might be

- scrapped (entirely)
- subjected to 100% inspection and faulty items scrapped
- sold as 'seconds' or
- reworked.

Discuss the pros and cons of these four alternatives in the case of a batch of chocolate bars rejected because too high a proportion of them were misshapen.

Exercise 5C

1. A manufacturing business analyses the credits given to its customers by the Sales Department. The results for 1995 and 1996 are given in the tables below.

1995

Cause	1st quarter No. Total value (£000)		2nd quarter No. Total value (£000)		3rd quarter No. Total value (£000)		4th quarter No. Total value (£000)	
Wrong product	1	20.3	2	35.7	0	0	1	17.8
Faulty product	10	5250	15	8375	9	4750	6	5025
Invoice error	27	9347	35	12712	27	13583	33	36395
Damaged	3	45.2	1	12	1	11.3	2	36
Short delivery	5	26	3	76	2	12.4	5	55
Processing error	4	17	6	42	4	7.4	5	57.3
Delivery error	3	29	2	13	2	15	4	58.5

1996

Cause	1st quarter No. Total value (£000)		2nd quarter No. Total value (£000)		3rd quarter No. Total value (£000)		4th quarter No. Total value (£000)	
Wrong product	1	17.9	12	211.4	19	300.6	14	318.8
Faulty product	9	5165	15	8775	12	7321	19	10914
Invoice error	11	6901	19	12712	12	7583	8	4299
Damaged	2	29.2	5	71.3	9	113	15	249.3
Short delivery	7	79	13	172	6	22.4	6	87.9
Processing error	5	36	4	25	2	13.4	1	3.7
Delivery error	17	181	15	150.5	12	129	3	33

(i) Produce a Pareto analysis of the credit notes for each year, according to the number of occurrences of each cause. Based on this analysis what would be your recommendations? In what way(s) do the analyses for 1995 and 1996 differ?

(ii) Produce a Pareto analysis for each year based on the value of the credit notes for each cause. What would be your recommendations now?

(iii) Correcting an invoice or other record involves only administrative time. Correcting or replacing faulty products usually involves more substantial costs, such as materials, transport, warehousing, labour and machine costs. The company estimates the average correction cost for each cause as follows.

Cause	Estimated average cost of correction (£)
Wrong product	500
Faulty product	4150
Invoice error	10
Damaged goods	100
Short delivery	45
Processing error	10
Delivery error	500

Produce a Pareto analysis for each year based on these estimates. How would this analysis affect your recommendations?

2. An electrical retailer buys resistors from a specialist supplier in batches of 1000. The retailer requires that no more than 1% of the resistors are faulty. He adopts a double sampling scheme with an initial sample of size 50. He decides to

- accept a batch if there are no faulty resistors in the initial sample
- reject a batch if there are 4 or more faulty resistors in the initial sample
- take a second sample of 50 if the first sample contains 1, 2 or 3 faulty resistors
- reject the whole batch if there are any faulty resistors in the second sample.

(i) Investigate this scheme for batches containing up to 5% faulty resistors. Do you think it is a satisfactory scheme?

(ii) Suggest an alternative scheme and explain why you think it will work better.

(iii) For the retailer's scheme and your own, calculate the average number of resistors inspected when the percentage of faulty resistors is 0.05%, 1% and 2%.

3. A machine produces components. A small proportion, p, are defective. The components are stored in large batches. The quality control operation consists of taking a sample at random from each batch and inspecting each component in the sample. The number of defective components in a sample is assumed to follow a Poisson distribution so that

$$P(r \text{ defectives in a sample size } n) = \frac{e^{-np}(np)^r}{r!}$$

(i) Consider a single sampling procedure in which a sample of size n_0 is drawn and the whole batch is accepted if c_0 or fewer

defectives are found, otherwise it is rejected. Show that the probability that a batch is accepted is

$$\sum_{k=0}^{c_0} \frac{e^{-n_0 p}(n_0 p)^k}{k!}$$

Evaluate this probability for the case $p = 0.01$, $n_0 = 20$, $c_0 = 1$.

(ii) Consider a double sampling procedure. First a sample of size n_1 is drawn. If there are c_1 or fewer defectives, the whole batch is accepted; if there are more than c_2 defectives (where $c_2 > c_1$), the whole batch is rejected. If neither of these holds, a further sample of size n_2 is drawn and the whole batch is accepted if there are c_2 or fewer defectives altogether, otherwise it is rejected. Show that the probability that a batch is accepted is

$$\sum_{k=0}^{c_1} \frac{e^{-n_1 p}(n_1 p)^k}{k!} + \sum_{k=c_1+1}^{c_2} \left\{ \frac{e^{-n_1 p}(n_1 p)^k}{k!} \sum_{l=0}^{c_2-k} \frac{e^{-n_2 p}(n_2 p)^l}{l!} \right\}$$

Evaluate this probability in the case $p = 0.01$, $n_1 = 4$, $c_1 = 0$, $n_2 = 16$, $c_2 = 1$.

(iii) For the situation of part (ii), show that the probability that a second sample is needed is

$$\sum_{k=c_1+1}^{c_2} \frac{e^{-n_1 p}(n_1 p)^k}{k_1}$$

Denoting this probability by P, deduce that the average sample size for this procedure is $n_1 + n_2 P$. Evaluate this for the case given at the end of part (ii).

(iv) Use your numerical results from the ends of parts (i), (ii) and (iii) to discuss briefly whether the single or the double sampling procedure is best for this particular situation.

KEY POINTS

After working through this chapter you should
- understand how to form and interpret Pareto charts and apply the 80% rule
- know how to apply and assess single- and double-acceptance sampling schemes using the operating characteristic curve
- be able to calculate the average number of items sampled in an acceptance sampling scheme.

6

Control charts

No process without data collection; no data collection without analysis; no analysis without action.

The diameter of a hole drilled in a car engine block is classed as a *critical dimension*: if it is not within a specified range of values, the engine will not work correctly. Rather than waiting to see if the car runs satisfactorily once the engine is fitted, it is sensible to check the diameter of the hole immediately after it has been drilled. What inspection procedures can be adopted to help minimise the number of engines produced with the hole incorrectly sized?

Using final inspection as a means of improving the quality of a model has been likened to steering a ship by looking at its wake. It may prevent large numbers of unsatisfactory products being sent out of the factory, but it does nothing to reduce the number of faulty items produced. When there are several stages in the production of the final item, a better approach is to use control charts. Control charts provide a method of monitoring important aspects of the production process, so that swift action can be taken if things start to go wrong. They help people to understand the process, and they almost always lead to improvements in the quality of a final product.

HISTORICAL NOTE

Control charts were first introduced by the American, Walter A. Shewhart in the 1920s. For this reason, they are sometimes called Shewhart *charts. They were popularised by W.E. Deming in Japan after the Second World War. Since the 1980s companies in the USA and the rest of the world, led by the Ford Motor Company, have adopted the charts as a standard part of their quality control.*

Variables or attributes?

To use control charts, you first need to identify the main stages in the production of an item, and then to decide which aspects of the item are to be checked at each stage. Sometimes the aspect to be checked cannot easily be measured: the item may either conform or not conform to the requirements. For example, it might be clean or not clean, straight or not straight. Other inspections, like checking the diameter of the hole drilled in a car engine block, will involve measurements. In these cases the data may take any of a whole range of values: you can record not only whether the item is conforming or non-conforming, but how far it is from the target value.

CIS

In order to set up new control charts in situations like this it is usual to use 100% inspection, so that the necessary process data can be gathered as quickly as possible. It might be decided that 20 samples of size 5 should be taken. From these data, the mean and the standard deviation for the process can be estimated, as well as the mean range of the samples. It is also important to find out whether the process is capable of producing items within the required tolerances, and whether the distribution of the sample means is Normal.

If the means and the ranges of the samples are recorded and plotted, you can make an assessment of whether the process has been operating correctly. If some values are much larger or smaller than others, you should try to determine the cause of these.

As you have seen, there are two basic sources of variability: common causes and special causes.

Common causes are present when the process is operating normally. They include many sources of minor variability. They are usually
• stable
• relatively predictable
• permanent (unless action is taken).

Special causes are unusual ones: they are not expected during normal operation. They tend to be individual major sources rather than combinations of more minor ones. They are usually
• irregular
• unpredictable
• liable to reappear unless action is taken.

If a reason can be found for an unusually large or small value, it has an assignable cause. If that cause can be removed, the extreme value may be removed from the data when it comes to estimating the parameters of the distribution. If an assignable cause cannot be found, the value should be retained in the calculations. Examples of assignable causes are a machining tool breakage, non-conforming input material and an operator's sudden illness.

Suppose that once any extreme values due to assignable causes have been removed from the initial data there are m samples, each of size n.

From the means, $\bar{x}_1, \dots, \bar{x}_m$ you may estimate the mean of the process:

$$\hat{\mu} = \bar{\bar{x}} = \frac{\sum\limits_{i=1}^{m} \bar{x}_i}{m}$$

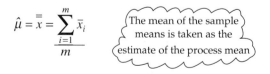
The mean of the sample means is taken as the estimate of the process mean

From the ranges, $r_1, \dots, r_m$ you may estimate the mean range of the process.

$$\bar{r} = \frac{\sum\limits_{i=1}^{m} r_i}{m}$$

The mean of the sample ranges is taken as the estimate of the true mean sample range.

The standard deviation could be estimated directly by pooling the standard deviations of the individual samples (see *Statistics 5*):

$$\hat{\sigma} = \sqrt{\dfrac{\displaystyle\sum_{i=1}^{m} ns_1^2}{m(n-1)}} \quad \text{where} \quad s_1^2 = \dfrac{\displaystyle\sum_{j=1}^{n} (x_{ij} - \bar{x}_i)^2}{n}.$$

Alternatively, the standard deviation could be estimated from the mean of the ranges of the samples by dividing by the appropriate value from the table below.

Sample size	2	3	4	5	6	7	8
Divisor	1.128	1.693	2.059	2.326	2.534	2.704	2.847

For example, if the mean of the ranges of samples of size 5 is 1.8 mm then the estimate of the standard deviation is $\dfrac{1.8}{2.326}$ mm.

An easier way to estimate the mean and the standard deviation of the process is to use a Normal probability plot. Such a plot is usually used to check that the sample means are Normally distributed, and so no extra work is involved. (For details of Normal probability plots see Appendix A.)

If the resulting estimate of the mean of the process is not the same as the target value for the item being produced, the machine is usually adjusted so that this is the case.

From the estimate of the standard deviation, the capability index of the process may be calculated using the usual formula

$$C_p = \dfrac{\text{upper tolerance limit} - \text{lower tolerance limit}}{6\sigma}.$$

If the capability index is unsatisfactory, in other words if it is less than 1.33 or 1.67 (depending on the policy of the firm) there is a major problem. If the capability study is being done prior to purchasing a machine, this result will probably prevent the purchase from going ahead. If an existing machine is being used to produce a new type of component, it is necessary to go back to the component designer, to see whether the tolerances can be altered or whether other components can be redesigned to cope with the variability. If none of these options is viable, it might be necessary to purchase a new machine that is capable of producing the component to the designer's specification.

If the distribution of the means turns out to differ appreciably from a Normal distribution, it might be necessary to

- try increasing the sample size, since according to the Central Limit Theorem, as $n \to \infty$ the distribution of sample means tends to the Normal distribution
- try transforming the data to obtain a Normal distribution, for example by taking logarithms
- try to fit another standard distribution to the data or
- continue to collect data from the process and estimate the control limits from the data.

The advantage of the distribution of the means being Normal is that this is a standard distribution and so the percentage points are easily found from tables. If the data needs to be transformed in order to obtain a Normal distribution there is an increased possibility of error.

Exercise 6D

1. The measurements in the table were taken on the initial production run of a process which shaped and pierced a component for a car air bag. The component was critical to driver safety, so its dimensions had to be monitored.
   (i) Plot the means and ranges and decide on suitable warning and action lines for the control charts.
   The design specification is 2.5 ± 0.05 mm.
   (ii) Do you believe that the process is capable of producing satisfactory items?

Time	Item number				
	1	2	3	4	5
11:30	2.51	2.51	2.50	2.50	2.51
11:45	2.50	2.51	2.51	2.52	2.52
12:00	2.51	2.51	2.51	2.51	2.51
12:15	2.51	2.51	2.51	2.51	2.51
12:30	2.48	2.49	2.49	2.48	2.48
12:45	2.50	2.50	2.50	2.50	2.50
13:00	2.49	2.49	2.50	2.50	2.49
13:15	2.50	2.50	2.50	2.50	2.50
13:30	2.49	2.49	2.50	2.50	2.49
13:45	2.50	2.50	2.50	2.50	2.50
14:00	2.51	2.50	2.50	2.50	2.51
14:15	2.51	2.51	2.51	2.51	2.51
14:30	2.50	2.50	2.51	2.50	2.50
14:45	2.50	2.50	2.50	2.50	2.50
15:00	2.51	2.51	2.50	2.50	2.50
15:15	2.51	2.51	2.51	2.51	2.51
15:30	2.51	2.50	2.50	2.51	2.51
15:45	2.51	2.51	2.51	2.51	2.51
16:00	2.51	2.51	2.51	2.51	2.51
16:15	2.50	2.51	2.51	2.50	2.50

CuSum charts

When there is particular concern about the possibility of a process moving away from the target value, it may be better to use a *CuSum chart* rather than a Shewhart means chart. A CuSum chart, as its name suggests, records the cumulative sum of the deviations from the target value.

Suppose that the following sequence of values has been obtained for the means of samples of size 5, where the target value is 15.000.

Sample no.	1	2	3	4	5	6	7	8	9	10
Mean	15.020	15.003	14.995	15.016	14.993	15.008	15.011	15.006	14.998	15.019

The corresponding Shewhart means chart is shown in figure 6.10.

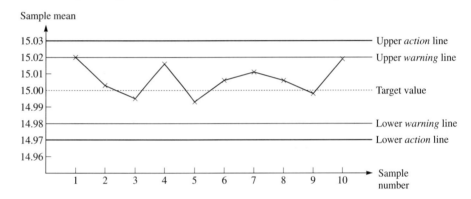

Figure 6.10

To produce the CuSum chart, you calculate the deviation from the target value, 15.000, as shown in the table below, and then work out the cumulative sum for each successive sample.

Sample no.	1	2	3	4	5	6	7	8	9	10
Deviation	0.020	0.003	−0.005	0.016	−0.007	0.008	0.011	0.006	−0.002	0.019
Cumulative Sum	0.020	0.023	0.018	0.034	0.027	0.035	0.046	0.052	0.050	0.069

You plot the cumulative sums of the deviations from the target value against the sample number, producing a CuSum chart as in figure 6.11.

Introduction to time series

You can never plan the future by the past.

Edmund Burke, 1729–97, British politician

Look at the three graphs below. What information can you obtain from them which would help you to forecast future values?

a)

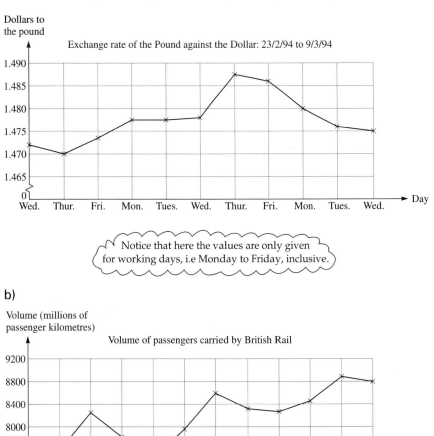

Dollars to the pound

Exchange rate of the Pound against the Dollar: 23/2/94 to 9/3/94

Notice that here the values are only given for working days, i.e Monday to Friday, inclusive.

b)

Volume (millions of passenger kilometres)

Volume of passengers carried by British Rail

Annual Abstract of Statistics. These figures are quarterly totals.

c)

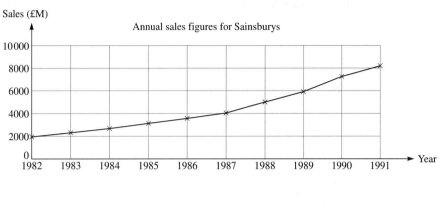

Whenever someone records a sequence of measurements, and the times at which they are taken, the result is a time series. The measurements recorded in a time series may be 'snapshots', as is the case for the exchange rate data. Alternatively they may be totals over a sequence of time periods: the British Rail figures are quarterly totals, and the Sainsbury figures are annual totals. The graphs of time series, such as those shown above, are called simply *time series plots*, or sometimes *historigrams* (not to be confused with histograms) because they give the history of the data.

The time series that you meet in this book, and most of the time series used in industry or commerce, are for data recorded at regular intervals.

We shall usually represent the time series by

$$y_0, y_1, y_2 \cdots y_t \cdots$$

The first value, y_0, is taken at time $t = 0$, the second, y_1, at time $t = 1$, and so on. For example, if we were tracking the value of the pound against the dollar at hourly intervals during a day, y_0 could be the value at 0900, y_1 the value at 1000 and so on. Alternatively, if we were investigating the sales of a certain product, y_0 might be the value of the sales in January, y_1 the value of the sales in February, … , and y_{12} would represent the sales in the following January. (An alternative notation, which is helpful in some situations, is to call the first term y_1.)

Why study time series?

The aim of recording and analysing a time series is usually to try to forecast future values of the variable, which will then be used in planning. For example, a manufacturing firm may need to forecast sales figures in order to plan its production schedules, or in order to organise warehouse space for the products.

Another reason for studying time series is to seek to understand a situation or process. For example, a time series plot of the sample means of measurements taken on a production line may be used to assess the capability of the process to meet the design specification (see Chapter 6).

Features of time series

Many of the features commonly associated with time series are illustrated in the three time series plots at the start of this chapter.
- The exchange rate time series shows quite a lot of variability and no stable overall pattern
- The passenger figures show a general upward trend, together with a seasonal pattern
- The Sainsburys figures show some variability, together with a clear upward trend.

Of course, if you were to look at these same variables over other different time periods you could well end up with quite different time series.

Although the three plots have few obvious similarities, there are certain important features that occur in many different situations.

Trend

A trend is a general, underlying movement of the measurements in one direction, either upwards or downwards. This movement may be obscured by random variation in the measurements, or by more systematic variation, such as seasonal factors. The sales figures and the passenger figures both seem to show a clear upward trend. By contrast, the exchange rate figures show no clear pattern or trend.

Stationarity

Time series which show neither an overall upward trend nor an overall downward trend are said to be stationary, or to exhibit stationarity. A stationary time series actually has a linear trend with zero gradient, but is sufficiently important to deserve study in its own right.

Seasonal variation

A seasonal pattern is one which repeats annually. Seasonal patterns can only be seen in data that are measured at intervals of fractions of a year. The British Rail passenger figures show a seasonal pattern: each year there is an increase from the first to the second quarter and another from the second to the third quarter, followed by decreases from the third to the fourth quarter and form the fourth quarter to the first quarter of the next year.

Cycles

A cyclical pattern is similar to a seasonal one; it is a recognisable, repeating pattern in the data. However, cycles do not necessarily have constant length. For example, businesses linked to the fashion trade may well experience cycles of varying length, associated with the emergence of a new fashion, its increase in popularity and its subsequent decline.

Random variation

Random variation is variation that does not appear to follow any particular pattern, and that we are unable to explain. If you can accurately identify any trends and seasonal or cyclical variations in a time series, the differences between the observed values and your forecast values should be due only to random variation (unless, of course, there is some other factor that you need to take into account).

Activity

(i)   For each of the three examples at the start of the chapter, state which standard features you can identify.
(ii)   Using only the information contained in the time series plots, try to forecast the next three values. In each case, indicate how confident you feel about the accuracy of your forecasts.

Exercise 7A

Plot time series for the following situations and identify any standard features that they exhibit. How confident would you be in attempting to forecast future values from each of these series?

1. Annual highs and lows of the Dow Jones industrial average on the New York stock-market from 1954 to 1985.

Year	1954	1955	1956	1957	1958	1959	1960	1961
High	404	488	521	521	584	679	685	735
Low	280	388	462	420	437	474	566	610

Year	1962	1963	1964	1965	1966	1967	1968	1969
High	726	767	892	969	995	943	985	969
Low	536	647	766	841	744	786	825	770

Year	1970	1071	1972	1973	1974	1975	1976	1977
High	842	951	1036	1052	892	882	1015	1000
Low	631	798	889	788	578	632	859	801

Year	1978	1979	1980	1981	1982	1983	1984	1985
High	908	898	1000	1024	1071	1287	1287	1360
Low	742	797	759	824	777	1027	1087	1185

2. The number of vehicles passing a point on a road during the morning rush hour, between 8 am and 9 am, on successive days over a four week period.

Week	Mon	Tues	Wed	Thur	Fri	Sat	Sun
1	1731	1667	1690	1757	1661	713	317
2	1639	1642	1660	1709	1657	774	342
3	1671	1622	1697	1723	1635	672	361
4	1684	1612	1639	1689	1652	685	311

3. The minimum monthly temperature over
a period of three years.

Year	Jan	Feb	Mar	Apr	May	June
1993	3.1	2.1	3.0	6.5	8.2	10.9
1994	1.3	–0.5	3.7	3.7	6.5	8.8
1995	0.3	2.8	0.3	3.7	5.2	8.2

Year	July	Aug	Sept	Oct	Nov	Dec
1993	11.6	10.3	7.4	4.5	0.8	2.1
1994	11.9	11.0	8.9	5.2	7.3	2.2
1995	12.3	11.8	8.5	8.9	3.0	–0.5

Smoothing a time series

Sometimes there is so much random or seasonal variation in a time series
that it is difficult to identify any underlying trends. In such cases you can try
to *smooth* the series to reduce the effects of the random or seasonal variation.
In this section you will see how to smooth series that have no seasonal component. Smoothing of time series that do have a seasonal component is covered in Chapter 8.

The closing value of a share over a three-week period (comprising fifteen
working days) has been recorded in the table below.

Day	0	1	2	3	4	5	6	7	8	9	10	11	12	13	14
Value (£)	1.32	1.45	1.49	1.38	1.72	1.51	1.67	1.30	1.82	1.48	1.84	1.75	1.57	1.81	2.08

NOTE

*In this case the first day has been labelled 'Day 0'. It would have been equally valid
to call it 'Day 1'. Either 0 or 1 may be used for the first observation. In some cases
there is a good reason for the choice and in others it is purely arbitrary.*

The time series plot is shown in figure 7.1.

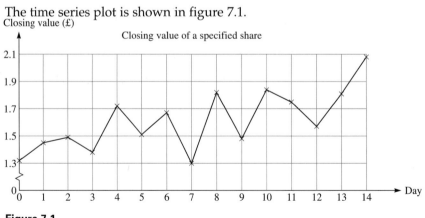

Figure 7.1

For Discussion

Can you identify an underlying trend?

If so, how would you go about modelling it so that it could be used for forecasting?

Try using your model to make some forecasts. How reliable do you think
they are?

There are several methods of reducing the 'scatter' (random variation) in a time series. Often they are used in conjunction with each other.

Moving averages

One method for smoothing a time series is to calculate a series of *moving averages*. For the time series

$$y_0, y_1, y_2, y_3, \ldots$$

you would calculate a 3-point moving average by working out the mean of each set of 3 consecutive values. The first value of the moving average would be

$$\frac{y_0 + y_1 + y_2}{3},$$

the second value would be

$$\frac{y_1 + y_2 + y_3}{3},$$

and so on.

You then plot each value of the moving average at the midpoint of the time period that it covers. So, for example, you plot the mean of y_0, y_1, y_2 at $t = 1$ and the mean of y_1, y_2, y_3 at $t = 2$.

NOTE

The terms 'moving mean' and 'moving average' are used interchangeably in this section. The term 'moving average' is used most often in practice.

Using the data on share values (table on p. 142) the first 3-point moving average would be

$$\frac{1.32 + 1.45 + 1.49}{3} = 1.42$$

and it would be plotted at $t = 1$.

The effects of using 3-point and 5-point moving averages on these data are shown in figure 7.2 (a) and (b).

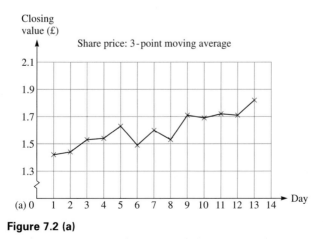

Figure 7.2 (a)

CIS

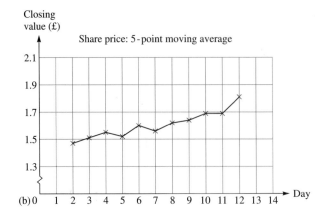

Figure 7.2(b)

In each case, the amount of variability in the data is reduced and an upward trend becomes more clearly visible. As you might have expected, the 5-point moving average has a greater smoothing effect than does the 3-point moving average. However, you need to ask yourself whether the moving average is showing you something that was really there in the first place. Is there really an increasing trend, or are the variations purely random? Looking back at the original time series plot, there does seem to be an increasing trend and it will be easier to model it from the moving averages than from the original data.

NOTE

There are two main purposes for smoothing a time series. The first is to try to see something in the data that was not immediately obvious on the time series plot. The second is to help us to model whatever we discover. Of course, once we have seen the feature (a linear trend, for example) in the smoothed series it may then appear to be fairly obvious in the original plot.

The next stage would be to try to fit a linear model to the smoothed time series. You would then check the validity of this by considering the residuals (the observed value minus the predicted value) as has been demonstrated previously. This is covered in Chapter 9.

Running medians

Running medians are very similar to moving averages. The 3-point running medians for the share data start with the median of 1.32, 1.45 and 1.49 which is 1.45. The second 3-point running median is the median of 1.45, 1.49 and 1.38 which is 1.45. Proceeding in this way, you can produce the graph in figure 7.3(a). The 5-point running median for the same data is shown in figure 7.3(b). (You can see that using an odd number of points makes the working very easy: running medians is an easier technique to use than moving averages if you are doing the working by hand.)

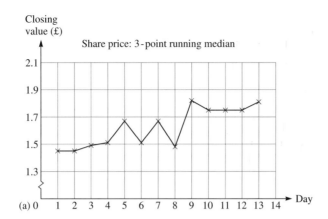

Figure 7.3 (a)

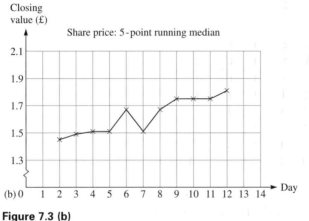

Figure 7.3 (b)

Again, after smoothing the time series, you would try to fit a model to the smoothed series and then check it by looking at the residuals.

The presence of an extreme value in the time series will have quite a large effect on the moving means that include it, but will have no effect on the running median values. The median is said to be *resistant* to outliers. Extreme values in the data could be due either to genuine large fluctuations or to errors in recording the data. If you want to prevent them from having a large effect on the smoothed series, you should use running medians rather than moving averages.

Weighted averages

When calculating moving averages, you can use a *weighted average* to give more emphasis to the middle value(s) than to the others. You can use any number of points, and choose any weightings you wish. A common approach is to calculate 3-point averages, and to give the middle one twice as much weight as the others. The first weighted average would then be

$$\frac{x_0 + 2x_1 + x_2}{4}$$

This particular system of moving averages is called *Hanning*.

The result of using Hanning on the share data is shown in figure 7.4.

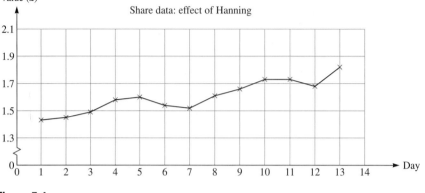

Figure 7.4

For Discussion

Compare the effects on the share price time series of moving averages, running medians and Hanning.

Do they all lead you to the same conclusion about an underlying trend in the share data?

It is possible to use these smoothing methods in combination. For example, you could use 3-point running medians to eliminate any extreme points, and then use Hanning.

Caution

As you have seen, smoothing methods do indeed reduce the variability in the data. The greater the number of points included in each average, the greater is the effect of the smoothing process. You might wonder whether a 7- or 10-point moving average could be used with even greater effect. However, any smoothing process loses some of the original information. Taking the argument to the extreme, you could use a 13-point moving average on the share figures, but then you would be left with only two points, which would be bound to lie on a line. Clearly, using 13 points is too extreme because you lose almost all of the original data.

Smoothing a time series will often give you greater insight into the data, and suggest a suitable model for the series. On some occasions, though, it may simply take you further and further away from the reality of the original time series. It is essential to use smoothing methods with caution, and to check any model that you obtain.

1. This table gives annual rainfall figures (mm) for England and Wales over the period 1950 to 1996.

   Use the methods from this chapter, singly or in combination, to investigate the figures and see if there is evidence of a climatic change. (Data kindly supplied by the Met Office.)

Year	1950	1951	1952	1953	1954	1955	1956
Rainfall	1014.9	1094.6	901.3	755.1	1092.5	773.4	865.2

Year	1957	1958	1959	1960	1961	1962	1963
Rainfall	903.9	1057.4	827.7	1194.8	905.2	813.8	877.9

Year	1964	1965	1966	1967	1968	1969	1970
Rainfall	725.3	1032.1	1061.1	1010.1	1095.3	905.3	934.4

Year	1971	1972	1973	1974	1975	1976	1977
Rainfall	824.4	853.4	739.9	1028.4	758.8	791.5	959.4

Year	1978	1979	1980	1981	1982	1983	1984
Rainfall	896.9	1023.3	967.2	999.8	989.4	885.4	929.7

Year	1985	1986	1987	1988	1989	1990	1991
Rainfall	892.9	1013.2	944.8	981.5	857.3	840.6	800.2

Year	1992	1993	1994	1995	1996
Rainfall	870.5	884.1	939.8	862.0	744.0

Introduction to time series

KEY POINTS

When you have worked through this chapter you should
- understand the meaning of the terms *time series plot, trend, stationarity, seasonal variation, cycle* and *random variation*
- know how to use moving averages and running medians to smooth time series.

8

Time series: formulating the model

Commercial and industral statistics

All models are wrong, but some models are useful.

George Box

Look at this time series plot for the quarterly sales figures (in tens of thousands of pounds) of a garden centre.

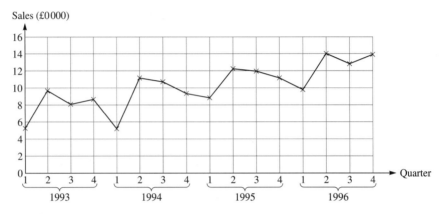

What sort of model do you think would fit these data?

How would you go about producing a model to enable the owner of the garden centre to forecast future sales?

The purpose of collecting and plotting time series data is often to produce a mathematical model for forecasting purposes. The model will usually be in the form of an algebraic expression. Each term in the expression represents one of the features of the time series. The coefficients give you an indication of the relative importance of the various terms, and thus of the features they represent.

To understand how this works, suppose that the first year's monthly sales of a magazine on computing have been recorded as a time series and that the series can be modelled by

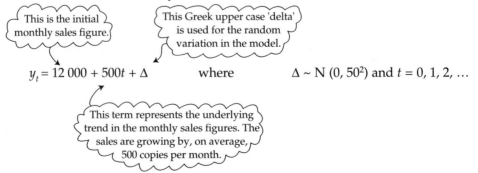

$y_t = 12\,000 + 500t + \Delta$ where $\Delta \sim N(0, 50^2)$ and $t = 0, 1, 2, \ldots$

This is the initial monthly sales figure.

This Greek upper case 'delta' is used for the random variation in the model.

This term represents the underlying trend in the monthly sales figures. The sales are growing by, on average, 500 copies per month.

The model is not *deterministic:* it does not produce exact values. The variability is represented by the random variable Δ, which in this case will usually lie between -150 and $+150$ (i.e. within three standard deviations of the mean). By substituting the appropriate values for t in this model, you can produce forecasts of the sales in future months. Substituting $t = 12$, for instance, will give you an estimate for the sales in the first month of the magazine's second year.

You will meet many more examples of time series models in the remaining chapters of this book. For each one, the values given by the model are compared with the actual recorded values, so that the performance of the model over the period for which data are available is used as a test of its reliability in the future. This is the best that can be done, since we cannot check it against the data for the future.

If a model successfully incorporates all of the features of the time series, the residuals (the differences between the observed values and the expected values) will consist only of random variation. It is sensible to calculate the residuals at each stage of the modelling process to see how well the model fits the data. If the residuals show a pattern, i.e. something which is predictable, you should try to incorporate this predictable feature into the model.

There is often scope for different interpretations of the same time series data, because a degree of subjectivity is involved. For example, what appears to you to be a linear trend may look to someone else like the beginning of a cycle, with a period of increase and then of decrease. As more data are collected, the features of the time series should become clearer.

Modelling procedure

The process of fitting a model to a time series, and using it, is illustrated in the next example. Many of the points arising from this example are developed in more detail in this chapter and the next.

EXAMPLE

The time series data for the monthly sales (in tens of thousands of pounds) of the garden centre mentioned on page 148 are given in the table below.

Year	1993				1994				1995				1996			
Quarter	1	2	3	4	1	2	3	4	1	2	3	4	1	2	3	4
t	1	2	3	4	5	6	7	8	9	10	11	12	13	14	15	16
Sales	5.26	9.66	8.09	8.66	5.20	11.17	10.72	9.34	8.85	12.24	11.96	11.16	9.79	14.02	12.82	13.90

In order to plan the purchasing and advertising schedule for the third and fourth quarters of 1997, forecasts of sales are required for that period. Using the data above, produce the required forecasts.

Solution

We start by plotting the series to see which model might be appropriate.

> Notice that this plot is the same one
> that appeared at the start of the chapter.

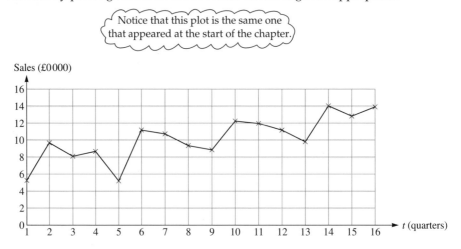

Sales (£0000)

The plot suggests that a suitable model would consist of a linear trend together with seasonal factors that are constant from year to year.

Using methods that will be developed later in this chapter and in Chapter 8, we find that the trend may reasonably be modelled by

$$y_t = 6.48 + 0.435t$$

This trend line is shown on the graph below together with the original time series plot.

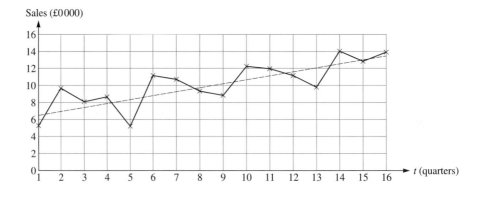

Sales (£0000)

The sales figures deviate above and below the trend line. Using the equation of the trend line, the sizes of the deviations can be calculated. They are shown in the following table and graph.

t	1	2	3	4	5	6	7	8	9	10	11	12	13	14	15	16
Sales value	5.26	9.66	8.09	8.66	5.20	11.17	10.72	9.34	8.85	12.24	11.96	11.16	9.79	14.02	12.82	13.90
$6.48+0.435t$	6.92	7.35	7.79	8.22	8.66	9.09	9.53	9.96	10.40	10.83	11.27	11.70	12.14	12.57	13.01	13.44
Deviation	−1.66	2.31	0.31	0.44	−3.46	2.08	1.20	−0.62	−1.55	1.41	0.70	−0.54	−2.35	1.45	−0.19	0.46

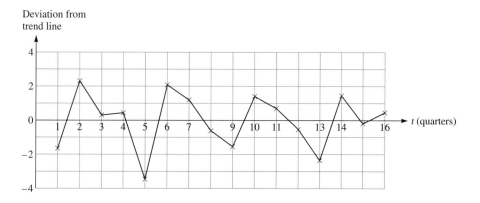

Deviation from trend line

The pattern seems reasonably stable from year to year. For example, the first quarter in each year has the lowest sales, and the second quarter has the highest.

The seasonal component in the model can be represented by q_i, a term which varies according to the quarter in question. The model is then written as

$$y = 6.48 + 0.435t + q_i$$

We now need values for q_1, q_2, q_3, and q_4.

The value of q_1 is calculated as the mean deviation for the first quarter:

$$\frac{(-1.65) + (-3.45) + (-1.55) + (-2.35)}{4} = -2.25.$$

The values of q_2, q_3, and q_4 are calculated in a similar way.

The complete set of these values is $q_1 = -2.25$; $q_2 = +1.81$; $q_3 = +0.50$; $q_4 = -0.07$.

The model is now $y_t = 6.48 + 0.435t + q_i$ with the values of q_i given above.

Using this, we obtain the forecast values shown in the table below.

t	1	2	3	4	5	6	7	8	9	10	11	12	13	14	15	16
Forecast sales	4.66	9.16	8.29	8.15	6.40	10.90	10.03	9.89	8.15	12.64	11.77	11.64	9.89	14.38	13.51	13.38

The observed values and the forecast values are shown in the graph below for comparison.

> For a more detailed treatment of seasonality see the section on *Modelling seasonal factors* pp 161–168.

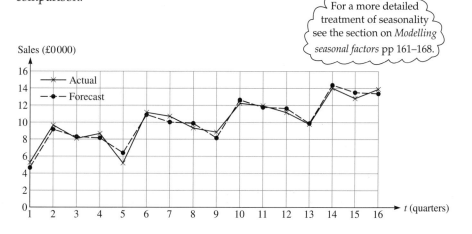

Sales (£0000)

The forecasts are close to the actual values, and so at this stage the model seems reasonable. It is always important to check the residuals (observed value minus forecast value), and these are plotted in the graph below.

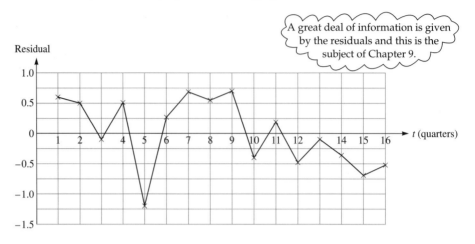

A great deal of information is given by the residuals and this is the subject of Chapter 9.

Since there is no obvious pattern in the residual plot, there is no reason to think that we have overlooked a predictable feature of the time series.

We obtain the forecasts for the third and fourth quarters of 1997 by calculating the trend at $t = 19$ and 20 and adding on the seasonal factors, +0.50 and −0.07.

The forecast sales for the third quarter are

The 'hat' shows that this is an estimate.

$$\hat{y}_{19} = 6.48 + 0.43 \times 19 + 0.50 = 14.795$$

and those for the fourth quarter are

$$\hat{y}_{20} = 6.48 + 0.43 \times 20 - 0.07 = 15.11.$$

To complete the model, an extra term, Δ, is required. This represents the random variation in the figures. From the plot of the residuals, we can see that in this case Δ varies between (roughly) −1 and +1. This indicates that the expected precision of our estimate is $\pm$ £100,000.

In the light of this, we might express the forecast sales as follows:

Quarter 3, 1997: between £700,000 and £900,000

Quarter 4, 1997: between £1,400,000 and £1,600,000.

The previous example showed you the process of fitting a model to data with a linear trend and constant seasonal variations. In the rest of the chapter you will meet other possible models, and see how to decide between them.

Models for the trend

This section concentrates on identifying and modelling trends in time series: it is assumed for the moment that there is no seasonal or cyclic component in the data.

Two models which have been found to be widely applicable for trends are the *linear model* and the *exponential model*. The linear model corresponds to growth (or decline) by a constant **amount** from one period to the next, whereas the exponential model corresponds to growth (or decline) by a constant **proportion** from one period to the next.

The linear model takes the form

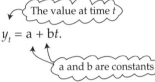

$$y_t = a + bt.$$

a and b are constants

This model fits time series in which the recorded values are a linear function of the time at which they were taken.

The values predicted by this model at times $t = 0, 1, 2, \ldots, n$ are $a, a + b$, $a + 2b, \ldots, a + nb$.

The basic exponential model takes the form

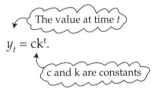

$$y_t = ck^t.$$

c and k are constants

The exponential model fits data that increase by a constant proportion, e.g. double or treble, for each unit increase in time. The values predicted by the exponential model for times $t = 0, 1, 2, \ldots, n$ are $c, ck, ck^2, \ldots, ck^n$.

NOTE *The basic exponential model may also be written as*

$$y_t = ce^{bt}.$$

This simply replaces k by another constant, e^b.

Using investigative plots to identify trends

In order to see whether the linear model or the exponential model provides a satisfactory representation of a particular time series, you can use a variety of *investigative plots*. These are described in turn below.

CIS

For each type of investigative plot, if it comes out as a (straight) line, that tells you something significant about the time series. You can judge quite well whether a graph is basically linear, whereas it is much more difficult to assess whether a graph is quadratic, cubic, sinusoidal or some other shape. A graph can be assumed to be linear if there is no obvious pattern in the deviations of the plotted points from a line.

There will be some time series for which a particular investigative plot tells you exactly what you want to know, and others for which that same plot tells you almost nothing.

If in the end your investigative plots suggest that neither the linear nor the exponential model is appropriate, they may at least give you an idea about how to proceed.

Time series plot

The first type of plot has already been mentioned. This is the time series plot. It is a plot of y_t against t. This enables you to look at the basic form of the time series and see which features you can recognise. In some cases this single plot may be all that is required. If not, the time series plot will often suggest which model may be appropriate, and which models are not appropriate.

Plot of differences

Sometimes the size of the figures makes it difficult to see whether the time series plot is basically linear. In such cases it is often helpful to plot the successive differences $(y_t - y_{t-1})$ against t.

If the time series data have been recorded on a regular basis, and if the increase each period is a constant (i.e. there is a linear trend), then the plot of differences will be a horizontal line.

The table below gives the population figures (in thousands) for Northern Ireland for the period 1958 to 1969. The corresponding time series plot is shown in figure 8.1

Year	1958	1959	1960	1961	1962	1963	1964	1965	1966	1967	1968	1969
Population	1402	1408	1420	1427	1437	1447	1458	1468	1476	1489	1503	1514
t	0	1	2	3	4	5	6	7	8	9	10	11

Annual Abstract of Statistics. Crown Copyright. Reproduced by permission of the Controller of HMSO and the Office for National Statistics.

Notice here that the first period has been called $t = 0$. In other cases you might decide to call the first period $t = 1$. Provided that you are consistent within any one time series, it does not matter.

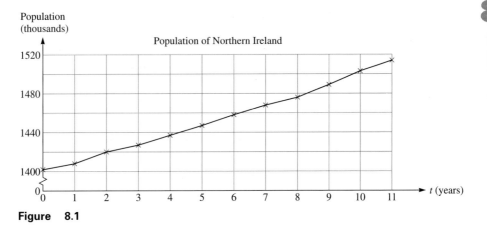

Figure   8.1

The graph appears to be reasonably linear, but it is not easy to be sure. You can check this by plotting the graph of the differences against *t*. The first step is to draw up a table of the differences.

t	1	2	3	4	5	6	7	8	9	10	11
$y_t - y_{t-1}$	6	12	7	10	10	11	10	8	13	14	11

The next step is to plot the differences against time, choosing a scale that is appropriate for the values in the table (see figure 8.2). This will have the effect of magnifying the deviations from a line.

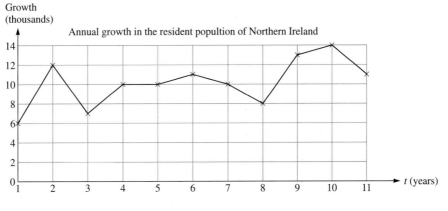

Figure   8.2

There is no obvious pattern here, and the differences are between 6 and 14 (thousand) which is relatively small compared with the values in the original series. There may be a slight upward trend, or the values could be fluctuating randomly about some constant value (roughly 10 000).

If you accept that the differences are stationary, i.e. that this plot has neither an upward nor a downward trend, then you can conclude that the linear model should be appropriate for the original time series. The resulting interpretation of the data is that the population of Northern Ireland was increasing during this period at a constant rate of about 10 000 per year.

CIS

There are several ways of going on to find the equation for the linear model:
- you can draw a line on the time series plot *by eye*
- you can calculate the *regression line* of y on t (see *Statistics 2*)
- you can find the *resistant line* (see Appendix C).

Your decision will depend on the precision required, the length of the time series, the availability of a calculator or a computer, the existence of outliers, and your personal preference. If the points lie very close to a line then all of the methods should give similar results. The use of the regression line is quite standard, but if some points are well above or below the line it would be worth considering using a resistant line.

If the plot of the differences has an upward trend, this shows that the amount of growth between time periods is increasing. If it has a downward trend, this shows that the amount of growth between time periods is decreasing. In either case, a linear model is not appropriate. To investigate the time series further, and to see whether an exponential model might be suitable, you could use a plot of ratios.

Plot of ratios

The formula for the exponential model is

$$y_t = ck^t.$$

Under this model, the ratio of successive values is

$$\frac{y_t}{y_{t-1}} = \frac{ck^t}{ck^{(t-1)}} = k$$

which is a constant.

Plotting $\dfrac{y_t}{y_{t-1}}$ (the ratio of successive values in a time series) against t

provides information about the relative growth from one period of measurement to the next. If the plot of successive ratios turns out to be approximately a horizontal line, the ratio of successive values is roughly constant, and the time series data can be modelled as having an exponential

trend. The value of k is given by the values of $\dfrac{y_t}{y_{t-1}}$. If the value of k is

greater than one, the model is one of exponential growth. If the ratio is less than one, the model is one of exponential decline.

To illustrate the use of a plot of ratios, the plot for the annual sales figures of Sainsburys, which you met on p. 139, is given in figure 8.3.

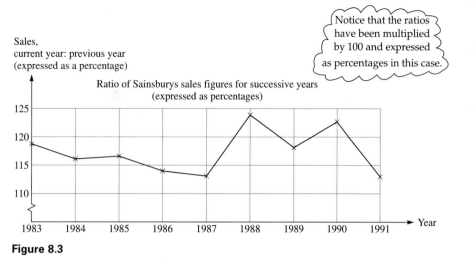

Sales,
current year: previous year
(expressed as a percentage)

Notice that the ratios have been multiplied by 100 and expressed as percentages in this case.

Ratio of Sainsburys sales figures for successive years
(expressed as percentages)

Figure 8.3

From the plot you can see that there was growth every year, since all of the percentages are greater than 100. You can also see that the greatest year-on-year growth was from 1987 to 1988 (about 24%) and that the smallest growth was between 1986 and 1987 (about 13%). There does not appear to be any overall trend.

You could conclude that the sales have grown by about 17% each year, with fluctuations about this value. It may, therefore, be possible to use the exponential model to represent this series.

The model would take the form

$$y_t = ck^t$$

and in this case $k \approx 1.17$.

Taking $t = 0$ for the first period (1982) gives

$$1950.5 \text{ million} = c.$$

The model becomes

$$y_t \approx 1950.5(1.17)^t$$

where y_t is measured in millions of pounds.

In Chapter 9 you will see how well this model fits the time series. At that point the precision of the model will also be discussed.

Plot of logarithms

Taking logarithms of the exponential model $y_t = ck^t$ gives

$$\log y_t = \log c + t \log k.$$

The graph of $\log y_t$ against t for the exponential model is therefore a straight line with gradient $\log k$ and intercept $\log c$.

Plotting $\log y_t$ against t for a set of time series data provides another way of investigating whether an exponential model might fit the data. If the plot of $\log y_t$ against t turns out to be basically linear, then the exponential model is

Time series: formulating the model

CIS

probably appropriate and you can estimate the parameters (c and k) from the plot:

- log k is given by the gradient of the plot
- log c is given by the vertical intercept of the plot.

Taking logarithms (to base 10) of the Sainsburys figures gives the figures in the table below. The plot of log y_t against t is shown in figure 8.4.

Year	1982	1983	1984	1985	1986	1987	1988	1989	1990	1991
Sales (£M)	1950.5	2315.8	2688.5	3135.3	3575.2	4043.5	5009.5	5915.1	7257	8200.5
Logarithm of sales (£M)	3.290	3.365	3.430	3.496	3.553	3.607	3.700	3.772	3.861	3.914

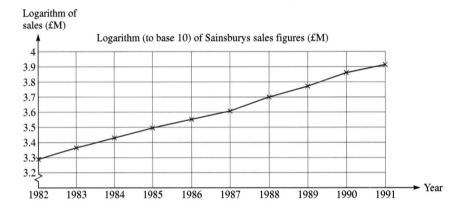

Figure 8.4

This graph is almost linear, and confirms that an exponential model should provide a good fit to the Sainsburys sales data.

A more general exponential model

You have already met the exponential model in the form

$$y_t = ck^t$$

where both c and k are positive constants.

The exponential model may be further generalised by adding a constant, and by allowing the coefficient of the exponential term to be negative as well as positive. The model becomes

$$y_t = c + ab^t \quad \text{where } b \geq 0.$$

The characteristics of the model depend upon the values of a, b and c.

- Altering the value of c simply moves the basic curve up or down: c defines the position of the horizontal asymptote
- if $0 < b < 1$, the curve moves towards the asymptote as t increases

- if $b > 1$, the curve moves away from the asymptote as t increases
- If $a > 0$, the curve is above the asymptote
- If $a < 0$, the curve is below the asymptote.

The various possibilities are illustrated in figure 8.5. The horizontal asymptote $y = c$ is included in each diagram.

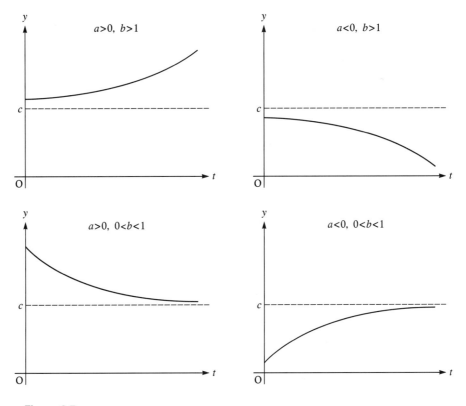

Figure 8.5

Fitting the general exponential model to a time series

In order to fit the more general form of the exponential model,

$$y_t = c + ab^t \quad \text{(where } b > 0\text{)},$$

to a time series, you need to estimate suitable values of a, b and c in the model. The easiest method is probably to estimate c as the value of the horizontal asymptote. (This may not be entirely straightforward, due to the random variation present in real data.) Subtracting c from each of the values in the series then produces a new time series with the horizontal axis as an asymptote. Calling these new values $y'_0, \ldots, y'_n$, you expect them to be modelled by the equation

$$y'_t = ab^t.$$

8

Taking logarithms now gives the familiar form

$$\log y_t' = \log a + t \log b.$$

Plotting $\log y_t'$ against t should therefore give a linear graph. The values of $\log a$ and $\log b$, and hence of a and b, can be estimated from the vertical intercept and the gradient, respectively.

Exercise 8A

1. For each of the examples at the start of Chapter 7, say whether you would consider a linear model or an exponential model, or whether you would completely reject both of these models.

2. The table shows the circulation figures per issue (in thousands) for a major regional newspaper. A time series plot suggests that a linear model might be appropriate.
   (i) Use a plot of differences to see if this initial idea is valid.
   (ii) If a linear model does appear to be appropriate, fit one and use it to forecast the sales for the next two years. What precision do you expect your forecasts to have? If a linear model appears inappropriate, suggest an alternative.

Year	1970	1971	1972	1973	1974	1975	1976	1977
Circulation	1457	1467	1452	1459	1446	1438	1422	1420
Year	1978	1979	1980	1981	1982	1983	1984	1985
Circulation	1413	1420	1361	1319	1284	1259	1259	1265
Year	1986	1987	1988	1989	1990	1991	1992	1993
Circulation	1266	1245	1234	1216	1213	1184	1197	1156

3. (i) Use a plot of ratios, and then a plot of logarithms, on the population data for Northern Ireland. How do your plots indicate that the growth is not exponential?
   (ii) Use a method of your choice to fit a linear model to the Northern Ireland population data.

4. Try using a plot of differences for the Sainsburys data. How does your plot indicate that the growth is not linear?

5. The table shows the quarterly sales figures for a special edition of a novel published in early 1994 to coincide with the release of the film based on the book. The sales in the first quarter after publication include all the bulk copies pre-ordered by shops, book clubs and overseas agents, so they are extremely high compared with the other figures.

   Ignoring the sales in the first quarter of 1994, fit an exponential model to the subsequent figures.

Year	1994				1995			
Quarter	1	2	3	4	1	2	3	4
Sales	668840	21911	15923	11703	9052	7232	5778	4913
Year	1996				1997			
Quarter	1	2	3	4	1			
Sales	4217	3613	3346	3340	3200			

6. Use a method of your choice to fit a linear model to the logarithm of the Sainsbury sales data.

Modelling seasonal factors

As you saw in the example on p. 151, seasonal patterns may be represented in a model by a term, q_i. In that example there were four values for q_i, one for each quarter. In this section you will see how to go about identifying and modelling any seasonal factors in a time series.

Very often a time series will show both a repeating, seasonal pattern and an underlying trend. If you can separate the seasonal effects from the underlying trend, you can model these two components separately and then add them together. Dealing with the two components of the model separately is easier than trying to deal with them both at once. One way of separating the components is the method of moving averages.

Seasonal data with no underlying trend

You have already used moving averages (or moving means) to smooth random variations in a time series. They can also be used to smooth seasonal variations, in order to see any underlying trend. To see how the method of moving averages works, look first at the table below, which shows the average daily sales of ice-cream cones from Jo's van.

	1990				1991				1992		
Spring	Summer	Autumn	Winter	Spring	Summer	Autumn	Winter	Spring	Summer	Autumn	Winter
300	1200	700	200	300	1200	700	200	300	1200	700	200

As you can see, the sales pattern is purely seasonal: the figures for Spring are the same each year, as are the ones for Summer, and so on. Clearly, it is very easy to predict Jo's average sales in this situation! The time series plot is simply a repeating pattern (see figure 8.5).

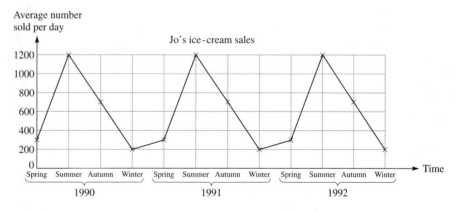

Figure 8.6

When using moving averages for smoothing out random effects in a time series, you can use any number of points in the moving average. The approach is different when you want to smooth out seasonal effects, because you need to use the same number of points in your moving average as there are time series points in a year. Since in this case the figures are recorded quarterly, a 4-point moving average is used.

$$\text{First average} = \frac{1}{4}(300 + 1200 + 700 + 200)$$

$$= 600.$$

$$\text{Second average} = \tfrac{1}{4}(1200 + 700 + 200 + 300)$$

$$= 600.$$

You have probably realised that for Jo's sales, because the data are purely seasonal, with no underlying trend and no other variations, the 4-point moving average is constant at 600. In any one-year period, Jo's mean daily sales are 600. The line corresponding to the mean has been plotted together with the time series in figure 8.7.

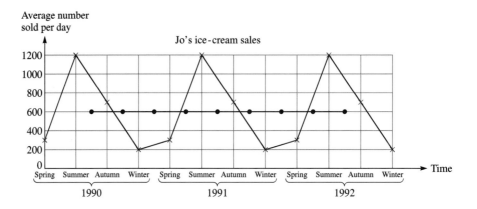

Figure 8.7

Having done this, it is useful to calculate the *seasonal deviations*: the amounts by which the sales for each season deviate from the overall mean.

For each season,

seasonal deviation = seasonal value – overall mean.

so for example, the seasonal deviation for Spring is

$$300 - 600 = -300.$$

The four seasonal deviations are shown in the table below.

Season	Spring	Summer	Autumn	Winter	Total
Seasonal deviation	–300	+600	+100	–400	0

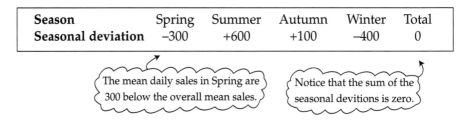

Notice that each value in the time series can now be expressed as the sum of the overall mean and the deviation for that season. For example

Spring value = overall mean (600) + seasonal deviation (–300) = 300.

Seasonal data with a linear trend

Now suppose that Kay, another ice cream seller, is making a steady impact on the market, as indicated by the figures below and the corresponding time series plot (figure 8.8).

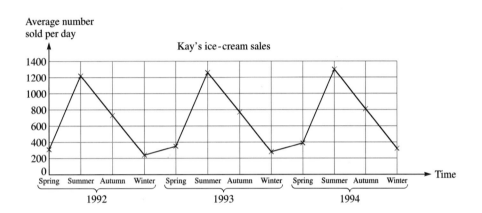

	1992				1993				1994			
	Spring	Summer	Autumn	Winter	Spring	Summer	Autumn	Winter	Spring	Summer	Autumn	Winter
	310	1220	730	240	350	1260	770	280	390	1300	810	320

Figure 8.8

In these data, as in the data for Jo's sales, the pattern recurs every four values so a 4-point moving average is used. You start by calculating the mean of the first four observations, then the mean of the second, third, fourth and fifth values, and so on. The results are as follows.

$$\text{1st mean} = \tfrac{1}{4}(310 + 1220 + 730 + 240) = 625$$

$$\text{2nd mean} = \tfrac{1}{4}(1220 + 730 + 240 + 350) = 635$$

$$\text{3rd mean} = \tfrac{1}{4}(730 + 240 + 350 + 1260) = 645$$

$$\text{4th mean} = \tfrac{1}{4}(240 + 350 + 1260 + 770) = 655$$

$$\text{5th mean} = \tfrac{1}{4}(350 + 1260 + 770 + 280) = 665$$

$$\cdots \qquad \cdots$$

$$\text{9th mean} = \tfrac{1}{4}(390 + 1300 + 810 + 320) = 705$$

To show the moving averages on the time series plot, you plot each one at the midpoint of the range to which it applies. For example, the first moving average corresponds to the first four observations and so you plot it half way between the second and third observations.

The original time series, the moving averages and the line through them are shown in the figure 8.9. You can see that in this idealised example the moving averages lie exactly on a line. With real data this will not be the case. If you think a linear model is appropriate for an underlying trend, you need to choose by eye or by some other method a line that fits the moving averages as well as possible.

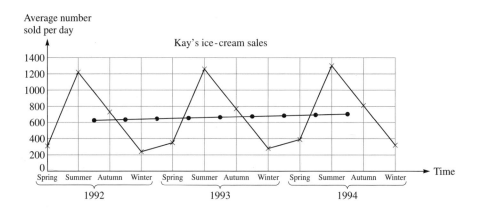

Figure 8.9

In this case you can verify directly from the graph that the seasonal deviations from the trend line are −300, +600, +100 and −400.

In a more complicated situation, you could find the equation of the line through the moving averages and then use this to calculate the seasonal deviations.

Activity

(i) For Kay's sales figures, calculate the equation of the *trend line*, the line through the moving averages.

(ii) Use your equation to calculate the trend value for each of the seasons covered by the original data, i.e. for each value of t.

(iii) Calculate the difference between each recorded value and the corresponding trend value. These are the seasonal deviations: check them against the values given in the text.

From the activity above, you can see that the time series can be decomposed into the form

$$\text{observation} = \text{trend line value} + \text{seasonal deviation}.$$

In this idealised case, the above relationship is satisfied exactly. This is because the trend is a perfect line and the seasonal deviations are exactly the same in each of the years.

In practice, even if the time series is quite clearly a seasonal pattern with an underlying linear trend, you do not expect the values to fit the model exactly. There will be extra factors, which you may not be able to model. For example, actual ice-cream sales will depend on the weather. During a particularly hot summer, sales might rise above the expected summer value, whereas a particularly cold and wet summer could cause sales to fall. If these factors can be identified and predicted, then they can be incorporated into the model and the model improved. If, on the other hand, they cannot be predicted, you have to accept the model and the larger variability.

To see how to go about modelling real data with a significant seasonal component, look at the British Rail passenger data below, and the corresponding time series plot shown in figure 8.10. (The figures are for the volume of passengers carried, measured in millions of passenger kilometers.)

Year	1986				1987				1988			
Quarter	Q1	Q2	Q3	Q4	Q1	Q2	Q3	Q4	Q1	Q2	Q3	Q4
t	1	2	3	4	5	6	7	8	9	10	11	12
Volume	7330	7583	8249	7822	7445	7961	8594	8318	8267	8459	8889	8797

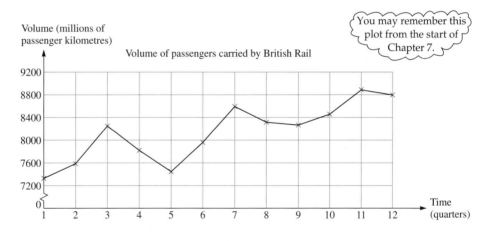

Figure 8.10

There seems to be a fairly clear seasonal pattern, with the volume of passengers carried increasing up to the third quarter and then decreasing to the next first quarter. As there are four quarters in a year, you can use a 4-point moving average to smooth the data. The results of this are shown in the table over the page.

t	2.5	3.5	4.5	5.5	6.5	7.5	8.5	9.5	10.5
Moving average	7746	7774.75	7869.25	7955.5	8079.5	8285	8409.5	8483.25	8603

Plotting these produces a graph which is approximately linear. This is shown in figure 8.11 along with the original points.

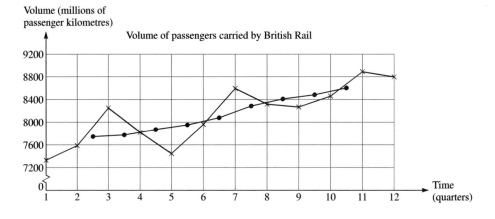

Figure 8.11

The moving averages have removed the seasonal component. The trend, which remains, appears fairly linear. The next step is to find the equation of the trend line.

Assuming that the trend is linear, you can use regression to find a line of best fit. This gives

$$y_t = 7380 + 116t.$$

> As mentioned earlier, you could alternatively fit a line by eye, or find the resistant line (see Appendix C).

The coefficients could have been given to several decimal places, but this does not seem reasonable given the size of the actual values and the variability in the data.

Using this equation, a table can be drawn up showing the trend value for each time period, and the difference between the actual value and the trend value.

Year	1986				1987				1988			
t	1	2	3	4	5	6	7	8	9	10	11	12
Actual volume	7330	7583	8249	7822	7445	7961	8594	8318	8267	8459	8889	8797
Trend value	7496	7612	7728	7844	7960	8076	8192	8308	8424	8540	8656	8772
Actual – predicted	-166	-29	+521	-22	-515	-115	+402	+10	-157	-81	+233	+25

The difference between the actual values in the time series and the values predicted by the trend line are plotted in figure 8.12 and show a seasonal pattern. The next step is to try to model this seasonal pattern.

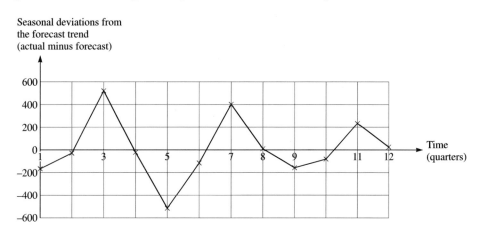

Figure 8.12

The highest values, which occur in each of the third quarters, appear to be decreasing. The values for the fourth quarter appear to show a slight increase. The other quarters do not appear to show any clear pattern.

This does not appear to be a simple pattern of constant seasonal deviations like that found in Kay's ice cream sales figures. You need to decide whether to try to model this more complex pattern or to make a simplifying assumption that each seasonal deviation may be adequately modelled by a constant. In this case, let us proceed by assuming that the seasonal deviations may be modelled by a constant.

To estimate the seasonal deviations for Spring, you use the mean of the deviations for Spring, and similarly for the other quarters. The estimates are shown in the table.

Season	Spring	Summer	Autumn	Winter	Total
Deviation	-279	-75	+385	+4	+35

Notice that, unlike in Kay's figures, the seasonal deviations do not sum to zero. You could make this so by subtracting 8.75 from each of the seasonal deviations and adding 8.75 to the constant in the model of the trend. However, compared with most of the seasonal deviations, 8.75 is not a large amount, and so no adjustment will be made at this stage. It is one of the things that you would consider if you decided to refine the model further.

For Discussion

What factors do you think might be responsible for this pattern of seasonal deviations?

At this stage you should check your model by looking at the residuals, and if you accept the models you can estimate the precision of any forecasts by considering the size of the residuals. These techninques are covered in detail in Chapter 9.

Using the model for forecasting

In order to use the model for forecasting, you simply substitute the appropriate value for t into the trend line equation

$$y_t = 7380 + 116t$$

to obtain the trend value, then add on the appropriate seasonal component, q_i.

EXAMPLE Use the model above to estimate the volume of passengers carried by BR (in millions of passenger kilometres) in the third quarter of 1989.

Solution

The third quarter of 1989 would correspond to time period 15. The trend value is therefore

$$y_{15} = 7380 + 116 \times 15 = 9120$$

The seasonal component for the third quarter is $q_3 = +385$.
The estimated volume is therefore

$$9120 + 385 = 9505 \text{ million passenger kilomeres.}$$

Exercise 8B

1. Use the model to forecast the values for the four quarters of 1994. Intuitively, how precise do you expect these to be?

2. The table below gives the maximum daily temperature, averaged over each month, for a period of three years.

Year	Jan	Feb	Mar	Apr	May	June	July	Aug	Sept	Oct	Nov	Dec
1993	9.4	6.6	11.0	13.5	17.0	20.9	20.6	20.5	16.5	11.9	7.8	8.3
1994	8.4	6.5	11.3	12.1	15.0	20.0	24.7	21.3	16.5	14.3	12.5	9.4
1995	8.1	9.5	9.8	13.6	17.4	19.6	24.8	26.1	17.9	16.8	10.8	4.3

   (i)   Decompose it into a linear trend plus seasonal deviations.
   (ii) Calculate the residuals and plot them against time.
   (iii) Does the residual plot tell you anything about the appropriateness of your model?

   (iv) Forecast the next two values in the series and estimate the precision of these forecasts.

3. The following table gives the quarterly consumers' expenditure figures for the UK in the years 1992 to 1995. The figures are adjusted to 1990 prices, which allows for the effect of inflation over that period.

Year	1992				1993			
Quarter	1	2	3	4	1	2	3	4
Expenditure	80765	82371	87191	89325	82763	83747	89556	91949
Year	1994				1995			
Quarter	1	2	3	4	1	2	3	4
Expenditure	85012	85917	91849	94136	86893	88202	93137	95813

Annual Abstract of Statistics. Crown Copyright. Reproduced by permission of the Controller of HMSO and the Office for National Statistics.

   (i)   Plot the time series. Does a linear model seem reasonable for the underlying trend?

(ii) Use a suitable moving average and plot the averages on your time series plot.

(iii) Find the line of best fit through your moving averages. You may do this just by eye or by using the regression formula. Plot the line on a graph and give the equation.

(iv) Calculate the deviations of the original points from the trend line.

(v) Use the means of the deviations for each quarter to estimate the seasonal deviations.

(vi) Calculate the values which your model gives for the period covered by the data and then find the residuals.

(vii) Plot the residuals against the time.

(viii) Plot the actual value against the values predicted by your model.

(ix) Comment on how well or badly your model fits the data.

(x) Use your model to forecast the value for the first quarter of 1996.

Other seasonal models

When modelling seasonal data, the aim is to separate the trend from the seasonal deviations. You have seen how this is done when the various effects are assumed to be *additive,* that is when the model has the form

$$y_t = m_t + s_t + \Delta_t$$

where m_t represents the trend, s_t represents the seasonal component and Δ_t represents the random variation. (We actually used q_i for the seasonal component previously, because the figures were quarterly.)

In fact, there are two other possible forms of seasonal model:

$$y_t = m_t.s_t . \Delta_t$$

and

$$y_t = m_t. s_t + \Delta_t.$$

Both of these models assume the seasonal effect to be *multiplicative:* the observed value is assumed to be the product of the trend and the seasonal component. This sort of model is appropriate when the seasonal factors appear to be percentage increases, or decreases, in trend value. In the first alternative the random component is also multiplicative; in the second the random component is additive.

The first of the alternative models may be transformed to an additive model by taking logarithms:

$$\log (y_t) = \log (m_t) + \log (s_t) + \log (\Delta_t).$$

This version of the model could then be fitted to the data in the same way as the additive model.

The other multiplicative model is much more difficult to deal with as it cannot be transformed to an additive model. We shall not develop it in this book.

For Discussion

You have already seen an additive model fitted to the British Rail passenger data. Look again at the British Rail time series plot. Do you think that a multiplicative model might fit the data better?

The additive model that you saw fitted to the British Rail passenger data assumes
- a linear trend
- seasonal components that are constant from year to year
- a random component that is Normally distributed about zero, with constant variance, and that is independent of previous random components.

This is the simplest type of seasonal model. It is also possible to assume a non-linear (e.g. exponential) trend, and to assume different forms of seasonal and random components, but these models will not be developed in this book.

Exercise 8C

1. (i) A model of the form $y_t = m_t s_t \Delta_t$ has been found to fit a data set perfectly. What is the value of Δ_t in this case?

   (ii) A model of the form $y_t = m_t s_t + \Delta_t$ has been found to fit a data set perfectly. What is the value of Δ_t in this case?

   (ii) What would be the value of the random term if the passenger numbers for a particular time period turned out to be 4% below the forecast provided by the trend and the seasonal factor?

2. The numbers of passengers carried by an airline on one popular route are modelled quite well by $y_t = m_t s_t \Delta_t$ where the symbols have their special meaning and the trend is linear.

   (i) What would be the value of the seasonal component for the first quarter if the passenger numbers were found to be 20% below the trend value for that quarter?

3. Two seasonal time series showing quarterly data with a linear trend and very small random variations are noticed to be more-or-less identical in the first year. One of the series can be modelled using an additive model and the other using a multiplicative model, each with seasonal components that are constant from year to year.

   How would you tell from their time series plots which was which?

KEY POINTS

After working through this chapter you should
- be able to use investigative plots to see whether a linear or exponential model is suitable for an underlying trend in a time series
- know how to estimate the parameters for linear and exponential models
- be able to smooth a seasonal time series using a suitable moving average
- be able to fit an additive seasonal model with a linear trend to an appropriate time series
- recognise when to adopt a model in which the seasonal effects are multiplicative rather than additive.

Checking and using the model

Don't expect, inspect.

Four different time series plots are shown below. They are similar in that they all start at about 800 and rise to about 900 as t increases from 0 to 49. A linear model has been fitted to each time series, and the resulting residual plots are shown.

In which cases would you be happy to use the fitted models and in which cases would you want to improve the models?

For the models that should be improved, how would you seek to do this? (Remember to look at the size of the residuals compared to the size of the data.)

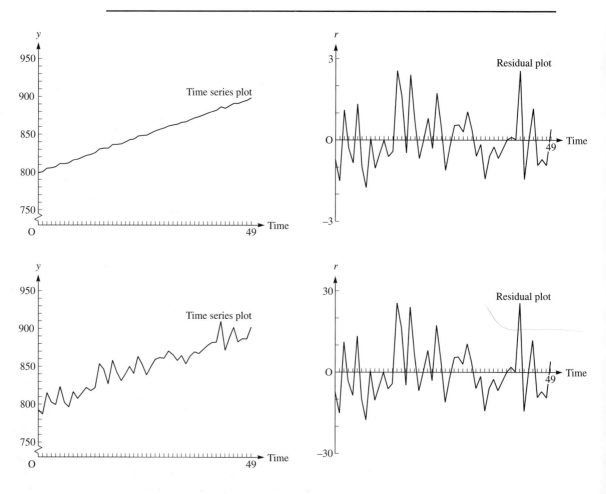

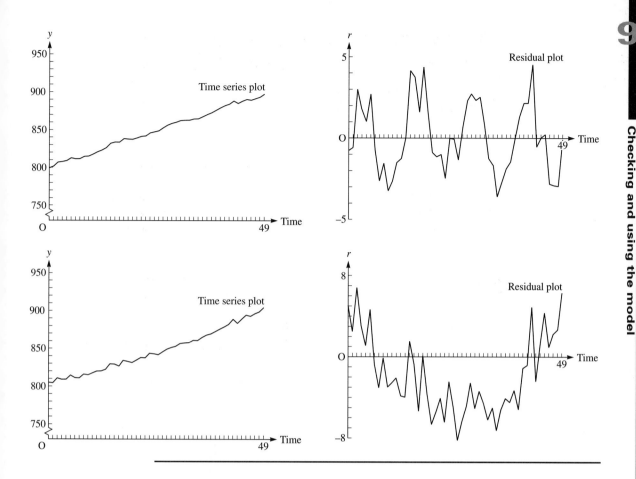

Checking the model

In order to test the validity of a time series model, you compare the values predicted by the model with the values in the data. You are looking at how well the model fits the existing data before using it to forecast future values. Clearly, the longer the time series, the more likely it is that you have identified the main features of the time series.

The residuals are the differences between the actual data values and the predicted values. The forecast values are sometimes called the fits, so you can write

data = fit + residual.

Suppose that the data values are $y_0, \ldots, y_n$ and the values forecast by the model are denoted by $\hat{y}_0, \ldots, \hat{y}_n$. The residuals $\delta_0, \ldots, \delta_n$ are given by

$$\delta_t = y_t - \hat{y}_t,$$

Clearly, if the model fits the data well the residuals will be small. If this is the case, it means that the model works well over the period for which you have data. It does not guarantee that the model will continue to work well in the future, but it does give you some confidence in the model.

In order to assess a model, you will usually make three plots. The first will be a plot of the expected values against time, superimposed on the original time series plot. The second will be a plot of the residuals against time (δ_t against t).

The third will be a plot of the observed values against the expected values (y_t against $\hat{y}_t$).

Figure 9.1 shows the time series plot for the British Rail passenger data from Chapter 8, together with the values predicted using the model developed on pp. 165–168.

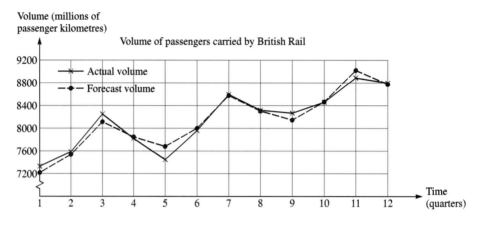

Figure 9.1

You can see that the model does in this case fit the data quite well: the expected values are in most cases very close to the actual values.

In the residual plot, you want the points to appear random. If there is some identifiable pattern in the residuals, such as a quadratic, you should try to incorporate this into your model, thereby improving it. Figure 9.2 shows the residuals for the model for the British Rail passenger data. They show no obvious pattern, so the residual plot gives you no cause to modify the model.

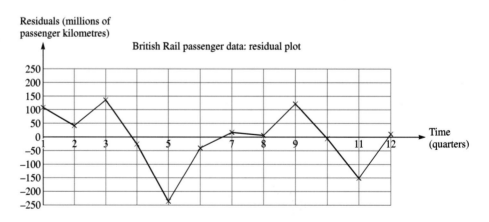

Figure 9.2

In the plot of y_t against $\hat{y}_t$, you want the two sets of points to be near the line of equality ($y_t = \hat{y}_t$).

The plot of the observed values against the forecast values is shown in figure 9.3.

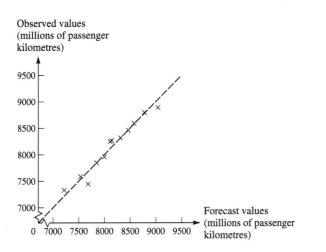

Observed values
(millions of passenger
kilometres)

Forecast values
(millions of passenger
kilometres)

Figure 9.3

The two case studies that follow illustrate how this works for a time series with a linear trend (the Northern Ireland data) and for a time series with an exponential trend (the Sainsburys data).

Case 1 (Linear trend)

The table shows the resident population of Northern Ireland over the period 1958 to 1969. You may remember meeting these figures in Chapter 8 (p. 154). The corresponding time series plot is shown in figure 9.4.

Year	1958	1959	1960	1961	1962	1963	1964	1965	1966	1967	1968	1969
Population	1402	1408	1420	1427	1437	1447	1458	1468	1476	1489	1503	1514

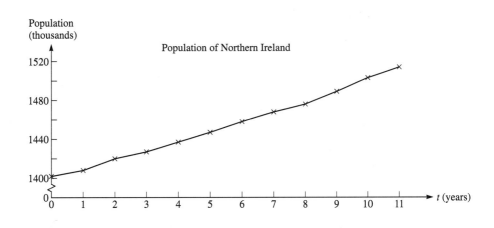

Figure 9.4

In Chapter 8 a plot of differences was used to show that a linear model would fit this time series well. The least squares regression line for the series is

$$\hat{y}_t = 10.2t + 1398.$$

The fits and the residuals are shown in the table below.

Year	1958	1959	1960	1961	1962	1963
t	0	1	2	3	4	5
Population	1402	1408	1420	1427	1437	1447
Fit	1397.95	1408.16	1418.36	1428.57	1438.77	1448.98
Residual	4.05	−0.16	1.64	−1.57	−1.77	−1.98
Year	1964	1965	1966	1967	1968	1969
t	6	7	8	9	10	11
Population	1458	1468	1476	1489	1503	1514
Fit	1459.19	1469.39	1479.60	1489.81	1500.01	1510.22
Residual	−1.19	−1.39	−3.60	−0.81	2.99	3.78

The agreement is very good indeed. To focus on the discrepancies rather than the agreement you need to look at plot of the residuals (figure 9.5).

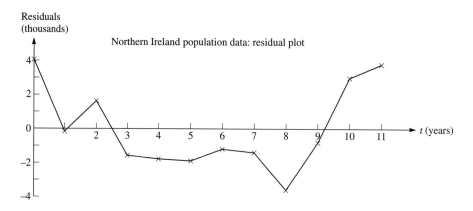

Figure 9.5

The residual plot suggests that there may be a slight curve in the time series plot, overlooked by the linear model. However, the residuals are very small when compared with the actual population – the largest residual value is 4050, compared with a total population of about 1.5 million – and so you would probably be fairly happy to use the model as it stands.

Case 2 (Exponential trend)

In Chapter 8 we investigated sales data from Sainsburys using a plot of ratios. The data were found to be well modelled by the exponential model

$$\hat{y}_t = 1950.5(1.17)^t.$$

This can be written in logarithmic form (using base ten) as

$$\log \hat{y}_t = 0.0682t + 3.290.$$

If $w_t = \log y_t$ and $\hat{w}_t = \log \hat{y}_t$, then, using this form of the model, the residuals are calculated from the equation

$$\delta_t = w_t - \hat{w}_t.$$

The actual and estimated values are given in the table, followed by the residuals. The time series data and the data estimated using the model are shown in figure 9.6.

Year	1982	1983	1984	1985	1986	1987	1988	1989	1990	1991
t	0	1	2	3	4	5	6	7	8	9
Sales (£M)	1950.5	2315.8	2688.5	3135.3	3575.2	4043.5	5009.5	5915.1	7257	8200.5
Log of sales (£M) $w_t = \log y_t$	3.290	3.365	3.430	3.496	3.553	3.607	3.700	3.772	3.861	3.914
Forecast of w_t $\hat{w}_t = \log \hat{y}_t$	3.290	3.358	3.426	3.495	3.563	3.631	3.699	3.767	3.836	3.904
Residual $\delta_t = w_t - \hat{w}_t$	0.000	0.007	0.003	0.002	-0.009	-0.024	0.001	0.005	0.025	0.010

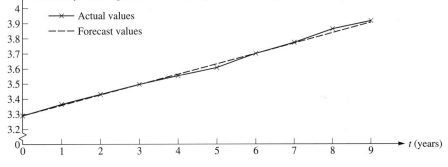

Figure 9.6

Clearly the model fits the (transformed) data extremely well. In order to focus on the discrepancies you plot the residuals against time, as in figure 9.7.

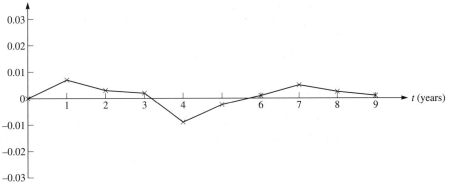

Figure 9.7

Does this plot increase your confidence in the model? The plot of the forecast values against the logarithms of the observed values is given in figure 9.8.

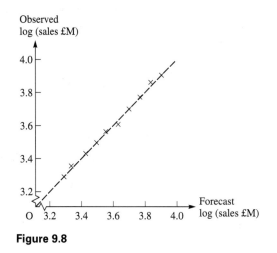

Figure 9.8

When is a model good enough?

As for any kind of mathematical modelling, the process of modelling a time series is an iterative one. You start by making simplifying assumptions, then produce a first, fairly simple model. You test it against the available data, and then modify the assumptions and revise the model if necessary. You could carry on doing this for many cycles, but at some point you need to accept that the model is good enough for your purposes, or reject it.

The point at which you decide to stop improving a model will depend upon
• the precision required in the model
• the amount of time and/or money available
• the amount of data available.

Sometimes the simplest model is actually adequate, because only a rough forecast is required. Sometimes you may have to be satisfied with a very poor model, because you cannot find a model that fits the data very well! This may be because you have not thought of the right model to use, or because there is a lot of random variation masking the underlying pattern.

Choosing between models

If you have two different models for a particular time series, how do you choose which to use? The first step is to look at the residuals from the two models. If one model gives much smaller residuals, that is the one to use. If the decision is not so clear, there are several possible criteria that you could use.
• Reject the model with the largest (absolute) residual
• Use the model with the smallest sum of absolute residuals

- Use the model with the smallest sum of squares of residuals, as in the least squares regression line.

Deciding which of these to use is a fairly subjective matter. It will depend in part upon the purpose for which the model is being developed.

Forecasting: point estimates

If in 1969 you had wanted to forecast the population of Northern Ireland in 1970 and 1971, you could have used the model on p. 176, i.e.

$$\hat{y}_t = 10.2t + 1398.$$

You could have substituted $t = 12$ and $t = 13$ into the equation, to produce a forecast population of 1.520 million in 1970 and 1.531 million in 1971.

As it turned out, the population was 1.527 million in 1970 and 1.540 million in 1971. The errors in your forecasts would have been 6.6 thousand and 9.4 thousand (0.43% and 0.61%, respectively). Comparing these with the previous residuals, reproduced in the table below, you can see that they are larger than any of them. This adds to the suspicion that there might be a slight upward curve in the time series.

Year	1958	1959	1960	1961	1962	1963	1964	1965	1966	1967	1968	1969
Residual	4.05	−0.16	1.64	−1.57	−1.77	−1.98	−1.19	−1.39	−3.60	−0.81	2.99	3.78

When a model is being used for forecasting, it is good practice to monitor the forecasts and to modify the model if necessary as more data become available. If you had needed in 1969 to make forecasts of the population figures for 1970 and 1971, the model would have been quite good, but the actual 1970 and 1971 figures might well have caused you to re-examine the assumption of a linear model and to see whether a quadratic or exponential model gave a better fit.

NOTE   *The method of fitting a parabola, say, to the data is similar to that used for fitting a line (see Statistics 6). The actual working can be made quite easy by using a computer spreadsheet or a specialised statistical package.*

For Discussion

What happens if you use the model to estimate the population for the years 1822 and 1823?

Does this mean that the first people arrived in Northern Ireland in 1822?

The discussion illustrates the dangers of *extrapolation* – using the model beyond the range of the data on which it has been formulated and tested. The model is based on data for the period 1958 to 1969, so using it to go back more than a century is almost bound to give silly results. The same would be true if you tried to use it to predict too far ahead.

Forecasting: interval estimates

For Discussion

A firm that stocks spare starter motors for a particular make of lorry needs an estimate of how many will be required each month. If it keeps too few, customers will be angry because they will have to wait for their order to be met, but if it keeps too many, it will have money tied up in excess stock and be wasting storage space.

Which is the more useful of the forecasts below?
(a) About 550 starter motors will be required next month.
(b) The number required will almost certainly be between 510 and 590.

At the beginning of Chapter 8 the model

$$y_t = 12000 + 500t + \Delta \quad \text{where} \quad \Delta \sim N(0, 50^2)$$

was used to represent the sales of a computing magazine. Since then we have focused mainly on modelling trends in the time series (represented in that case by $y_t = 12000 + 500t$) together with any seasonal effects. We have more-or-less ignored the random variation (represented in the computing magazine example by $\Delta \sim N(0, 50^2)$). The forecasts obtained so far have used the *deterministic* part of the model, and have therefore been *point estimates*. In order to have some idea of the likely precision of your forecasts you need to be able to say something about the random variation, using the *stochastic* part of the model. Knowledge of the random variation will enable you to produce *interval estimates*, which are much more informative than simple point estimates.

Modelling the residuals

Your ability to model the random variation will depend on the amount of data available and on how well your model fits the time series. At a very simple level you could pick out the largest residuals (positive and negative) and say that these define the likely limits of the error in your estimate. So, if your model of the trend produces an estimate of 2437 and the largest residuals are −5.8 and + 4.1, you may reasonably expect the actual value to lie between 2431.2 and 2441.1. You might give your forecast as 'between 2431 and 2441' or even as 'between 2430 and 2440'.

At the other extreme, if you had sufficient data and you found that the residuals were well modelled by a $N(0, 3^2)$ distribution, then you could give your forecast in the form of a confidence interval (*Statistics 3*). If your point estimate were 2437, a 95% confidence interval would be $2437 \pm 1.96 \times 3$ which is from 2431.22 to 2442.88.

NOTE

In fact, models can be developed which take into account the uncertainty in the estimates of the parameters of the model (for example, the slope and the intercept of a linear trend) when obtaining forecasts, but we shall not deal with them in this book.

Our knowledge of the random variation comes from looking at the residuals. The residuals are not exactly realisations of the random variable Δ, since Δ represents the deviations from the true model (assuming that there is such a thing) whereas the residuals are the deviations from the model that you have produced. Nevertheless, if your model fits the time series well and if the series is quite long then the residuals will give a good picture of the distribution of Δ.

NOTE *The situation is similar to one which you have met previously: with univariate data the variance of the sample (s^2) is measured from the mean of the data ($\bar{x}$) but we use it to estimate the population variance (σ^2) which is measured from the mean of the population (μ).*

A model which is often adequate for the random variation is $\Delta \sim N(0, \sigma^2)$. One major assumption in this model is that the form of the variation does not change over time, in particular that the variance remains constant. The assumption that the mean is zero is often satisfied, since when it is not the case it can be achieved simply by adding a constant to the model. One further assumption which is often made is that the value of Δ at time t is independent of the value at time $t - 1$.

All of these assumptions can and should be checked. The main tool to use is a plot of the residuals against time. This will indicate whether their mean is zero and their variance is constant. It may also indicate whether the values are independent, but this may be investigated further using the methods of Chapter 10. To check for a Normal distribution you could use a histogram, a stem-plot or a probability plot (see Appendix A).

To see how modelling the residuals can help in forecasting, we look again at Sainsburys sales figures.

The exponential model

$$\hat{y}_t = 1950.5(1.17)^t$$

has been seen to fit the data well. For the period covered by the data, it gives the results in the table.

Year	1982	1983	1984	1985	1986	1987	1988	1989	1990	1991
t	0	1	2	3	4	5	6	7	8	9
Sales (£M)	1950.5	2315.8	2688.5	3135.3	3575.2	4043.5	5009.5	5915.1	7257.0	8200.5
Forecasts	1950.5	2282.1	2670.0	3123.9	3655.0	4276.4	5003.4	5853.9	6849.1	8013.4
Residuals	0.0	33.7	18.5	11.4	-79.8	-232.9	6.1	61.2	407.9	187.1

The mean of the residuals is 41.3 and the standard deviation is 158.2.

If the Normal distribution is a reasonable model for the residuals then approximately 95% of residuals will lie within 2 standard deviations of the mean, i.e. between -275.1 ($= 41.3 - 2 \times 158.2$) and 357.7 ($= 41.3 + 2 \times 158.2$).

The sales forecast for 1992 in £M is

$$1950.5 \times 1.17^{10} = 9375.718\ldots$$

Using what we have just found about the residuals, you could forecast that the sales, in £M, would be between 9375.7 – 275.1 and 9375.7 + 357.7, i.e. between 9100.6 and 9733.4. You might reasonably express this in round figures as between 9100 and 9750 (£M).

If you needed to be more cautious, you could use the fact that almost all (99.73%) of the values in a Normal distribution lie within three standard deviations of the mean. The interval estimate would then be between 8942.4 and 9891.6 (£M). You might reasonably express this as between 8950 and 9900 (£M).

In fact, the Normal distribution does not fit these residuals terribly well. An alternative approach would be to use the residuals themselves to provide the limits of the interval estimate. The residuals range approximately from –230 to +410. Therefore a cautious forecast for 1992 would be between 9375 – 230 and 9375 + 410, i.e. between 9145 and 9785 (£M). By discounting the two most extreme residuals, you can say that 80% of them lie between –80 and +190, so a slightly less cautious interval estimate would be between 9375 –80 and 9375 + 190, i.e. between 9295 and 9566 (£M).

Exercise 9A

1. The graphs below are the plots of residuals against time after a model has been fitted to the trend of a time series.

In each case, say whether you would accept the model.

If you would accept the model, say how you would attempt to model the residuals.

If you would reject the model, say how you would seek to improve it or what alternative model you would try.

(b)

(a)

(c)

Exercise 9A continued

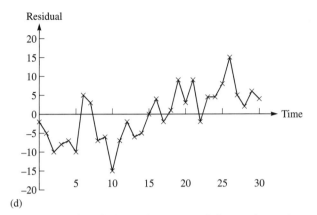

(d)

(i) Plot the time series and fit a seasonal model with a linear trend.

(ii) Use your model to forecast the figures for the next two months, giving some idea of the expected precision of your estimates.

Month	1	2	3	4	5	6	7	8	9	10	11	12
Sales	1202	1131	1574	1502	1810	2818	2517	1951	1639	1572	1832	1265

Month	13	14	15	16	17	18	19	20	21	22	23	24
Sales	1667	1429	1933	1701	2201	2189	3192	2364	1653	1807	1575	1343

Month	25	26	27	28	29	30	31	32	33	34	35	36
Sales	2031	1732	2585	1987	2916	3282	4158	4348	2308	2572	2011	2255

2. After fitting a linear model to a time series of 50 values, the plot of residuals against time suggests that their variance is constant, and a probability plot suggests that a Normal distribution provides a good model of the residuals. The model of the trend gives a forecast for the next value of 4238. The mean of the residuals is 0.3 and the standard deviation is 5.6. Use these figures to provide 90%, 95% and 99% confidence interval estimates instead of the point estimate.

3. The following table gives the monthly sales (in drums) of an industrial chemical.

(iii) The next two values turned out to be 2457 and 2128. Are they within your interval estimates?

4. The table below gives the monthly sales (in tonnes) of an industrial chemical. Plot the time series and, if appropriate, fit a seasonal model with a linear trend. Use your model to forecast the figures for the next year, giving some idea of the expected precision of your estimates.

Month	1	2	3	4	5	6	7	8	9	10	11	12
Sales	644	633	636	641	630	626	632	643	645	615	635	647

Month	13	14	15	16	17	18	19	20	21	22	23	24
Sales	633	636	633	638	619	628	635	646	637	629	627	646

Month	25	26	27	28	29	30	31	32	33	34	35	36
Sales	643	632	638	620	612	638	642	637	634	621	622	641

KEY POINTS

After working through this chapter you should
- be able to use the residuals to check the fit of a model to a time series
- be able to use the residuals to estimate the precision of a forecast
- be able to give interval forecasts when the random variation is adequately modelled by a Normal distribution.

9

Checking and using the model

We learn from history that we learn nothing from history.

The diagrams below show three different types of stationary time series. Can you identify the differences?

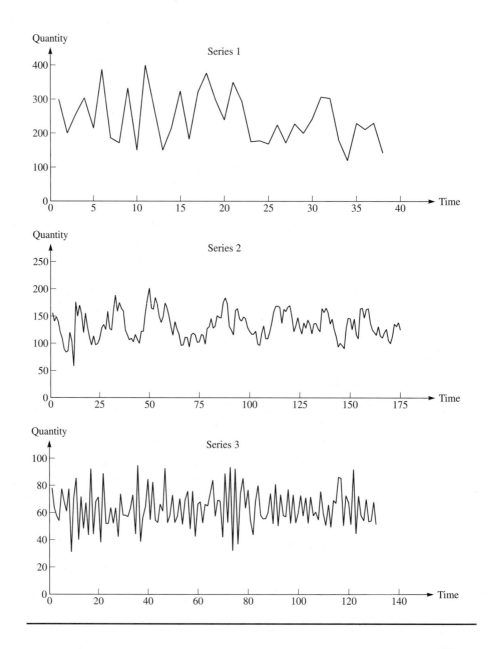

The differences between these time series may not be immediately obvious to you, but they are important.

In **Series 1** consecutive values are independent of each other. The variability is random. Knowing the current value is of no help in forecasting the next value. All you can do is use the data to estimate the mean, the range, the standard deviation and perhaps the distribution of the values.

In **Series 2**, there is a tendency for high values to occur together and for low values to occur together. The difference between one value and the next tends to be a smaller proportion of the range than in Series 1. This means that you can expect the next value to be similar to the current value, so the current value is a useful guide to forecasting the next one.

In **Series 3**, the data move up and down a great deal. If the current value is above the average then you can expect the next one to be below the average, indeed, if the current value is an extreme value, it will tend to be followed by a value at the other extreme. The current value is again a guide to forecasting the next one.

When the consecutive values in a time series are related to each other, rather than independent, we say that they are *autocorrelated*. If you have an autocorrelated time series, the current value gives you information about the likely value of the next observation, so you can use this fact in forecasting.

The time series plots on p. 184 are all stationary, i.e. there is no upward or downward trend. They represent reasonably stable situations such as the weekly demand for an established product. Series 2 shows a positive autocorrelation: it might represent a situation in which a high demand one week is likely to be followed by a high demand the next week. Series 3 shows negative autocorrelation: it might represent a situation in which a high demand one week tends to be followed by a low level of demand the following week.

For Discussion

Describe a real situation that you would expect to give rise to
(a) a positively autocorrelated time series
(b) a negatively autocorrelated time series.

If a sequence of values is positively autocorrelated, larger values tend to occur together, as do smaller values. If you plot on a scatter graph y_1 against y_0, y_2 against y_1, and so on, you should find that most of the points lie near to a line with positive gradient. On the other hand, if the sequence is negatively autocorrelated, such a plot should produce points lying near to a line with negative gradient.

The first 10 data points for Series 2 (positive autocorrelation) are given below.

t	0	1	2	3	4	5	6	7	8	9
y_t	158	141	149	142	119	110	88	83	86	120

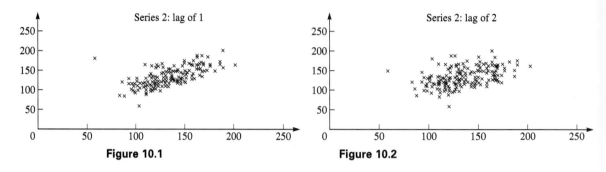

The plot for the whole series is shown in figure 10.1. The actual points plotted in this case are (141, 158), (149, 141), and so on. We say that the plot has a *lag* of 1, since each value is plotted against the value one step behind it: the second value is plotted against the first, the third against the second, and so on.

Figure 10.1

Figure 10.2

This plot shows quite a high degree of positive correlation. In fact, the Pearson's product moment correlation coefficient (which you met in *Statistics 2*) works out for these data as 0.67 (to 2 significant figures). This confirms what you can see from the graph, that high values tend to occur together, and low values tend to occur together.

If instead you plot the same data with a lag of 2, i.e. y_2 against y_0, y_3 against y_1 and so on, you obtain the plot shown in figure 10.2.

In this case, the correlation coefficient is 0.46. The data show some positive correlation with a lag of 2, but not so much as they showed with a lag of 1.

If each value in the time series is related to the one preceding it, then you would expect some kind of relationship, but perhaps a rather weaker one, with the value two before it in the series. The correlation coefficient confirms this.

The corresponding plots for lags of 3 and 4 are shown in figures 10.3 and 10.4.

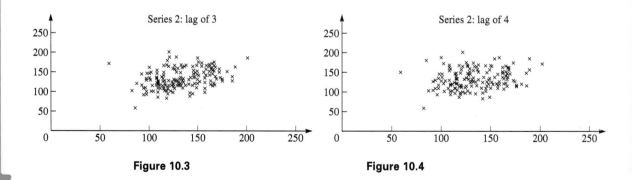

Figure 10.3

Figure 10.4

The correlation coefficients for these two plots are 0.35 and 0.22, respectively. The correlation is becoming weaker as we compare values that are further apart in the time series.

Figures 10.5 and 10.6 show the equivalent four plots for Series 1, where the values are independent, and for Series 3, where the values are negatively autocorrelated.

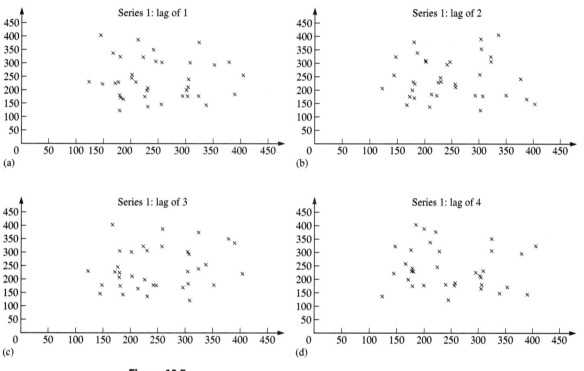

Figure 10.5

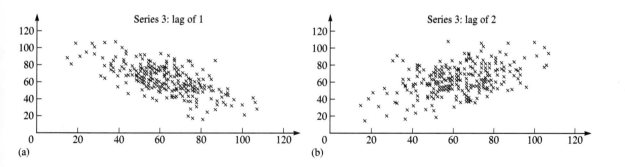

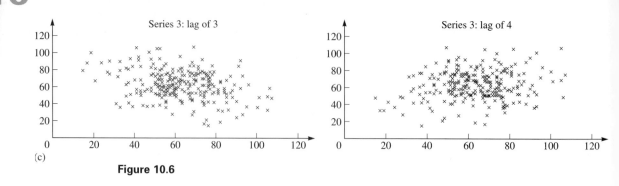

Figure 10.6

For Discussion

How do these differ from the plots showing positive autocorrelation?

Clearly, it is much easier and quicker to obtain these plots, and the value of the correlation coefficient, using a computer. Most statistical software packages, spreadsheets, databases and graphics calculators have facilities for this.

Exercise 10A

1. The first 16 data points for Series 3 (negative autocorrelation) are given in the table below. Plot the values against each other with lags of 1, 2, 3 and 4. Calculate the correlation coefficients in each case.

t	0	1	2	3	4	5	6	7
y_t	70	46	68	74	37	76	17	81
t	8	9	10	11	12	13	14	15
y_t	15	88	33	79	48	90	42	83

2. The first 16 data points for Series 1 (independence) are given in the table below. Plot the values against each other with lags of 1, 2, 3 and 4. Calculate the correlation coefficients in each case. (They are actually the monthly sales, in numbers of drums, of an industrial chemical.)

t	0	1	2	3	4	5	6	7
y_t	303	201	258	305	212	389	185	166
t	8	9	10	11	12	13	14	15
y_t	338	144	404	257	147	222	324	179

Correlograms

The information in the scatter plots is summarised by the correlation coefficients. A helpful way of looking at these is to plot the correlation coefficients against the lags. Such a plot is called an *autocorrelogram*, or simply a *correlogram*. It is tedious to do the work on a calculator, but many statistical computing packages will produce correlograms.

Figure 10.7 shows the correlograms for Series 1 (the independent values). Plotting with a lag of zero means plotting points against themselves, so it gives perfect correlation with a correlation coefficient of 1. This has been included to give a sense of scale and to facilitate comparisons with subsequent correlograms.

Correlation coefficient

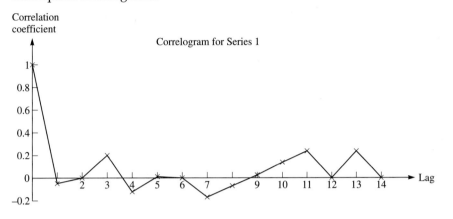

Figure 10.7

In this case the values of the product moment correlation coefficient are quite small, and they do not vary very much. This is no surprise, since the values in the time series are thought to be independent of each other and so the correlations plotted are those that arise between random points.

The correlogram for Series 2 (positive autocorrelation) is rather different. It is shown in figure 10.8.

Correlation coefficient

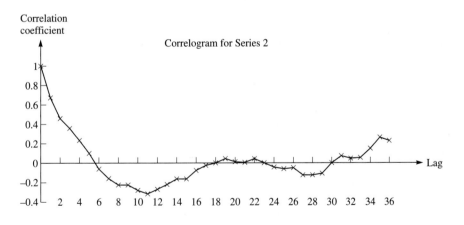

Figure 10.8

In this case, the first few correlation coefficients are positive and much larger than in Series 1. They decrease as the lag increases. Again this is no surprise, since the relationship is between adjacent points and so you would expect it to decrease as the interval between the points increases.

The correlogram for Series 3 (negative autocorrelation) is shown in figure 10.9.

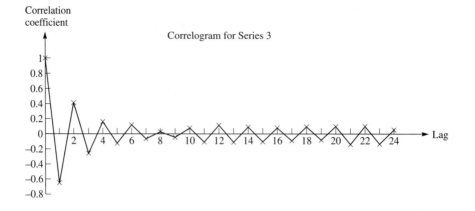

Figure 10.9

In this case, the first few values of the correlation coefficient are quite large compared with those obtained from the data showing independence, and they alternate in sign. As for Series 2, they tend to decrease in size as the lag increases.

For Discussion

Why does the correlation coefficient in Series 3 alternate in sign as you increase the lag?

Why does the correlation coefficient in Series 3 tend to decrease in size as the lag is increased?

NOTE

Every time you increase the lag, you decrease the number of points that can be plotted. Eventually you have only two points on the scatter graph, and these necessarily have a correlation coefficient of +1 or -1. If your time series has only a small number of points, you must be careful of working with too large a lag in order to avoid this spurious correlation.

Detecting seasonality using a correlogram

For Discussion

If the correlogram for a time series of quarterly data shows low correlation for lags of 1, 2 and 3 but a much higher correlation for a lag of 4, what does this suggest?

The time series plot in figure 10.10 is for the monthly sales of an industrial chemical. At first glance you might say that the series appears fairly stationary, and that the variation is random. However, the correlogram for these data is shown in figure 10.11. It tells a rather different story.

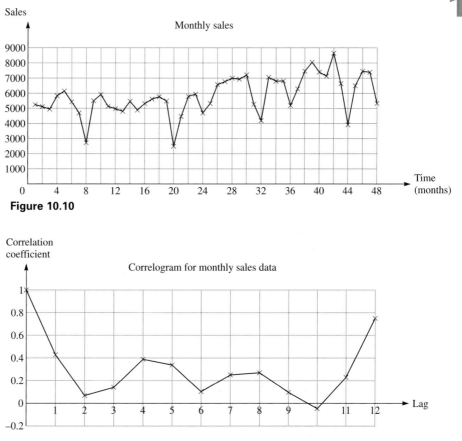

Figure 10.10

Figure 10.11

The correlation rises significantly at a lag of 12. The data values that are 12 months apart are strongly correlated. This reveals that there is a clear seasonal pattern in the data. When you are working with monthly or quarterly figures, you should always check whether there is an annual cycle (i.e. a seasonal pattern) like this. In the time series plot, as in the case above, the pattern may not be immediately obvious. Once a seasonal pattern has been detected, you carry on by modelling the data as in Chapter 8.

Correlograms may of course be used in a similar way to detect other cycles of constant length.

Forecasting when values are autocorrelated

When you have an autocorrelated time series, different methods of modelling and forecasting are needed to take the autocorrelation into account. Autocorrelation makes the methods more complicated but it does mean that your forecasts will tend to be more accurate than if successive values were independent.

Exponential smoothing

One method of forecasting autocorrelated series is called *exponential smoothing*. The greater the level of autocorrelation, the more reliable should be the forecasts using this technique.

There are several versions of exponential smoothing.
- *Single exponential smoothing* is used for forecasting from a stationary time series
- *Double exponential smoothing* is used for forecasting from a time series with a trend
- *Treble exponential smoothing* is used for forecasting from a time series with seasonal factors.

This book concentrates on single exponential smoothing for series with positive autocorrelation. Double and treble exponential smoothing are similar but more complex.

Single exponential smoothing

Single exponential smoothing uses a weighted average of the previous values in the time series to provide a forecast of the next value. The weights form a geometric progression and are chosen so as to give the greatest weight to the most recent values. The first term (the earliest value to be used in producing the forecast) is treated differently. The weight given to this is chosen so that the sum of the weights is 1. Usually the weight given to the earliest term will be quite small.

You should remember that a geometric progression is of the form

$$a, ar, ar^2, ar^3, \ldots, ar^{n-1}.$$

The nth term is ar^{n-1};

the sum of the first n terms is $G_n = \dfrac{a\left(1 - r^n\right)}{1 - r}$.

In single exponential smoothing, the first term of the geometric progression is usually denoted by the Greek letter α (alpha), which is chosen such that $0 \le \alpha \le 1$, and the common ratio, r, is put equal to $1-\alpha$. In this case,

$$G_n = \frac{a\left(1 - r^n\right)}{1 - r} = \frac{\alpha\left[1 - (1-\alpha)^n\right]}{1 - (1-\alpha)} = \frac{\alpha\left[1 - (1-\alpha)^n\right]}{1 - 1 + \alpha} = \frac{\alpha\left[1 - (1-\alpha)^n\right]}{\alpha} = \left[1 - (1-\alpha)^n\right].$$

To make the weights sum to 1, the earliest value used for the forecast is given the weight $(1 - \alpha)^n$. The pattern of weights used is as shown in the table below.

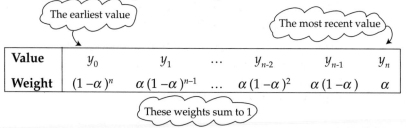

Value	y_0	y_1	...	y_{n-2}	y_{n-1}	y_n
Weight	$(1-\alpha)^n$	$\alpha(1-\alpha)^{n-1}$	...	$\alpha(1-\alpha)^2$	$\alpha(1-\alpha)$	α

Using these values, the forecast is

> The 'hat' indicates that this is an estimate of y_{n+1}.

$$\hat{y}_{n+1} = \alpha y_n + \alpha(1-\alpha)y_{n-1} + \alpha(1-\alpha)^2 y_{n-2} + \ldots + \alpha(1-\alpha)^{n-1} y_1 + (1-\alpha)^n y_0.$$

> It is customary to lay out the terms with the most recent value first.

To see how the technique works, let us return to Series 2, the time series with positive autocorrelation. The first sixteen values in the time series are given in the table below, together with the weights for use in exponential smoothing when $\alpha = 0.3$. The right hand column contains the data values multiplied by their appropriate weightings.

t	y_t	weight, w_t	$y_t w_t$ (to 3 d.p.)
0	158	0.7^{15}	0.750
1	141	0.3×0.7^{14}	0.287
2	149	0.3×0.7^{13}	0.433
3	142	0.3×0.7^{12}	0.590
4	119	0.3×0.7^{11}	0.706
5	110	0.3×0.7^{10}	0.932
6	88	0.3×0.7^{9}	1.065
7	83	0.3×0.7^{8}	1.435
8	86	0.3×0.7^{7}	2.125
9	120	0.3×0.7^{6}	4.235
10	103	0.3×0.7^{5}	5.193
11	59	0.3×0.7^{4}	4.250
12	180	0.3×0.7^{3}	18.522
13	149	0.3×0.7^{2}	21.903
14	172	0.3×0.7^{1}	36.12
15	150	0.3	45

> Notice that the more recent values are towards the foot of the table.

The estimate of the next value is now simply the sum of the entries in the right hand column:

$$y_{16} = 143.546\ldots$$
$$= 143.5 \text{ (to 1 decimal place)}.$$

If instead you use $\alpha = 0.1$, which gives less weight to the most recent observation, you obtain

$$y_{16} = 134.221\ldots$$
$$= 134.2 \text{ (to 1 decimal place)}.$$

Clearly the choice of α makes a considerable difference to the forecast obtained. If you take $\alpha = 1$ you are simply using the latest value as your forecast. If you take $\alpha = 0$ you are taking the initial value as your forecast.

The effect of the initial (earliest) value on the forecast will be quite large if either or both of the following apply:
• the series is short
• the value of α is near to zero.

If you are concerned about the possibly excessive influence of the initial value on the forecast, you can use the mean of the series as the initial value. In the example above, the mean of the series is 125.563. The values used in the calculation would now be as shown below.

t	y_t	weight, w_t	$y_t w_t$ (to 3 d.p.)
*	125.563	0.7^{16}	0.417
0	158	0.3×0.7^{15}	0.225
1	141	0.3×0.7^{14}	0.287
2	149	0.3×0.7^{13}	0.433
3	142	0.3×0.7^{12}	0.590
4	119	0.3×0.7^{11}	0.706
5	110	0.3×0.7^{10}	0.932
6	88	0.3×0.7^{9}	1.065
7	83	0.3×0.7^{8}	1.435
8	86	0.3×0.7^{7}	2.125
9	120	0.3×0.7^{6}	4.235
10	103	0.3×0.7^{5}	5.193
11	59	0.3×0.7^{4}	4.250
12	180	0.3×0.7^{3}	18.522
13	149	0.3×0.7^{2}	21.903
14	172	0.3×0.7^{1}	36.12
15	150	0.3	45

Notice that the series now has 17 terms.

The forecast value is now 143.4 (to 1 decimal place) which is almost the same as the 143.5 obtained previously.

Using this approach with $\alpha = 0.1$, you get a forecast of 128.2 (to 1 decimal place) which is different from the previous forecast of 134.2. Using $\alpha = 0.1$ puts greater weight on the first value in the series, so inserting the series mean at the start of the calculation has, as you would expect, a greater impact on the forecast in this case. Even with a series of only 16 terms, though, you can see that the effect of the first term is not large compared with the effect of the most recent terms.

Activity

For $\alpha = 0.1$, 0.2 and 0.3 calculate the weight for the terms y_n, y_{n-1} ... ,y_{n-5} and show your results in a table. Comment on the effect of the different values of α

Quicker methods of exponential smoothing

The amount of working involved in calculating successive estimates may be reduced considerably by rearranging the formula. The version which we have so far is

$$\hat{y}_{n+1} = \alpha y_n + \alpha(1-\alpha)y_{n-1} + \alpha(1-\alpha)^2 y_{n-2} + \ldots + \alpha(1-\alpha)^{n-1}y_1 + (1-\alpha)^n y^*$$

where y* is either the initial value of the series or the mean of the values in the series.

If you take out the factor $(1-\alpha)$ from all but the first term, you obtain

$$\hat{y}_{n+1} = \alpha y_n + (1-\alpha)\left[\alpha y_{n-1} + \alpha(1-\alpha)^1 y_{n-2} + \ldots + \alpha(1-\alpha)^{n-2} y_1 + (1-\alpha)^{n+1} y^*\right].$$

Since the expression in square brackets is an estimate of y_n, you now have the formula

$$\hat{y}_{n+1} = \alpha y_n + (1-\alpha)\hat{y}_n.$$

In other words,

forecast of next value = $\alpha \times$ present value

+ $(1-\alpha) \times$ forecast of previous value.

This form is very convenient for use with a calculator, since you can work from the initial value in the series, and at each stage you only need to know the forecast of the previous value, and the actual previous value in order to calculate the next estimate. This saves both memory space and calculation time.

Another useful rearrangement of the formula is

$$\hat{y}_{n+1} = \hat{y}_n + \alpha\left(y_n - \hat{y}_n\right).$$

In this form you can see that the forecast of the next value is the forecast of the previous value plus a correction factor based on the error in that forecast.

Using either of these shortened forms of the formula on the series above, putting y_0 as the starting value and $\alpha = 0.3$, you would start with $y_0 = 158$ and $\hat{y}_0 = 158$ and produce an estimate of y_1:

$$\hat{y}_1 = 158.$$

You should expect this, since the best estimate you can make of y_1 when all you know is that the initial value is 158, must be 158.

Now you use $y_1 = 141$ and $\hat{y}_1 = 158$ to obtain an estimate of y_2:

$$\hat{y}_2 = 152.9.$$

Proceeding in this way, you obtain the values in the table below. The values have been given correct to 2 decimal places, but you would keep all the decimal points on the calculator during the working.

t	0	1	2	3	4	5	6	7
y_t	158	141	149	142	119	110	88	83
$\hat{y}_t$	158	158	152.9	151.73	148.81	139.87	130.91	118.04
t	8	9	10	11	12	13	14	15
y_t	86	120	103	59	180	149	172	150
$\hat{y}_t$	107.52	101.067	106.75	105.62	91.64	118.15	127.40	140.78

Plotting this series of forecasts and the original series on the same graph we obtain figure 10.12. (The forecasts using the same approach but with $\alpha = 0.1$ are also shown for comparison.)

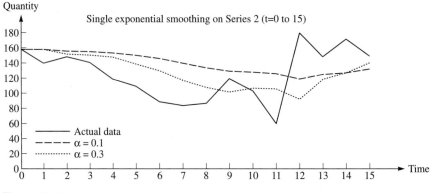

Figure 10.12

Both series of forecasts follow the original series, but they are much smoother.

As usual, before using a formula for forecasting, it is wise to look at the residuals and see how good your forecasts have been for the available data. The next table shows the residuals (correct to 2 decimal places) calculated from the table above, i.e. with $\alpha = 0.3$. Figure 10.13 shows the plot of the residuals against time

t	0	1	2	3	4	5	6	7
Residual	0	−17	−3.9	−9.73	−29.81	−29.87	−42.91	−35.04
t	8	9	10	11	12	13	14	15
Residual	−21.53	18.93	−3.75	−46.62	88.36	30.86	44.60	9.219

10

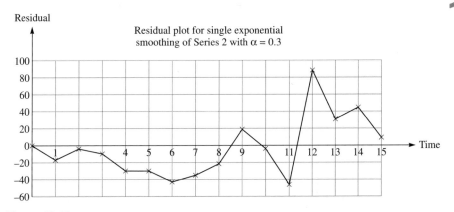

Residual

Residual plot for single exponential
smoothing of Series 2 with $\alpha = 0.3$

Time

Figure 10.13

There does not appear to be any pattern in this plot of residuals and so there
is no obvious predictable feature overlooked by the forecasting method.

Figure 10.14 shows the observed values plotted against the forecast values. If
the forecasts matched the actual values in the series, the points would all lie
on the line $y = x$. What this graph tells you is that the forecasts of low values
tend to be too high and the forecasts of high values tend to be too low.

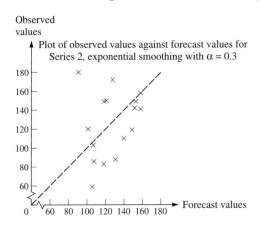

Observed
values

Plot of observed values against forecast values for
Series 2, exponential smoothing with $\alpha = 0.3$

Forecast values

Figure 10.14

For Discussion

Why does exponential smoothing produce estimates that are generally
closer to the mean than the actual values?

Activity

If you have access to a spreadsheet, use it to investigate the effects of
• the choice of α
• the length of the series
• the use of the mean as the initial value.

CIS

Choosing a value for α

The value you choose for α can have a very large effect on the forecasts produced by single exponential smoothing. When computing facilities are available, the following procedure may be used. Although it looks daunting, it is quite easy on a spreadsheet.

1. Choose an initial value for α.
2. Using this value of α, produce a forecast for each term in the series using the preceding values.
3. Calculate the residuals (observed value minus forecast value).
4. Calculate a suitable function of the residuals, such as their maximum value, the sum of their squares or the sum of their absolute values.
5. Vary α in order to minimise the chosen function.
6. Adopt the value of α which minimises the function, and therefore gives the 'best' fit to the known data values.

This procedure is equivalent to the method used for choosing between two models in Chapter 9.

Looking back to figure 10.12, you can see that the forecasts obtained using $\alpha = 0.3$ are generally closer to the actual time series than are the forecasts obtained using $\alpha = 0.1$.

Single exponential smoothing of the time series in Series 1 (the time series with independent values) produces forecasts that are more significantly affected by the value of α. This is shown in figure 10.15. The corresponding residual plots are shown in figure 10.16.

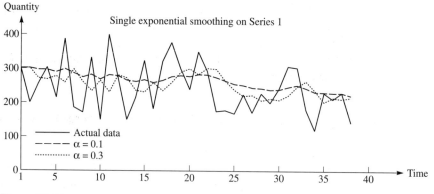

Figure 10.15

In this case, the residuals are smaller using $\alpha = 0.1$ than they are using $\alpha = 0.3$, so you would choose $\alpha = 0.1$. Can you explain this?

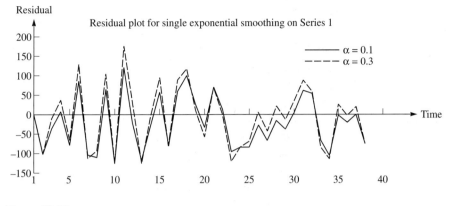

Figure 10.16

Interval estimates

As has been pointed out, when you are forecasting it is generally better to give an interval estimate than a point estimate. The size of the interval is determined from the residuals, since these show you how well your forecasting method has performed in the past.

If a Normal distribution is a reasonable fit to the residuals, you may use the confidence intervals associated with the Normal distribution (such as ± 2 standard deviations for an approximate 95% interval). If the Normal distribution is not a good fit then you need to use a dot-plot, stem-plot or histogram to look at the residuals and find the range within which most of them lie. You then use this to produce an interval estimate for the next value in the time series.

Applications of exponential smoothing

Exponential smoothing can be used for tasks such as stock control, where many time series are being handled and the forecasting is being done automatically by computer. It might not be possible in these circumstances for each time series to be investigated in detail, so a standard method is needed: it is more reasonable to assume that there will be autocorrelation than to assume that successive values will be independent. Of course, automatic forecasting packages are becoming increasingly sophisticated, and so more and more of them will include built-in checks for such features as autocorrelation.

Single exponential smoothing may only be used with **stationary** time series. If you use single exponential smoothing on a time series with a positive linear trend, the mean value of the series up to the current point pulls the forecast down.

10

Similarly, if single exponential smoothing is used on a time series with a negative linear trend, the mean value of the series up to the current point pulls the forecast up. Using a larger value of α ensures that the forecasts follow the series more closely, but the basic effect is the same.

As mentioned earlier, double exponential smoothing should be used for time series with a trend, and treble exponential smoothing should be used if there is seasonality. The theory behind these is beyond the scope of this book.

Exercise 10B

1. The personnel manager of a large manufacturing firm is concerned about the number of workers absent on any one day. In order to monitor this she records the number of people who are absent over a period of 15 weeks. The number of person days lost each week are recorded in the table below ('1 person day' means one person for one day, so 6 person days might mean 1 person is absent for 6 days, or 2 people for 3 days each, etc.).

Week	1	2	3	4	5	6	7	8
Person days	33	40	27	38	47	65	72	61

Week	9	10	11	12	13	14	15
Person days	58	26	31	29	31	40	37

(i) (a) Draw the time series plot for these data.

(b) Does the series appear to be autocorrelated?
(c) What is the correlation coefficient with a lag of 1?
(d) Why might the series be expected to be autocorrelated?

The manager wishes to try to forecast the number of absentees in order to decide when extra temporary staff need to be employed.

(ii) (a) Use exponential smoothing with $\alpha = 0.3$ to produce estimates starting from week 1, and plot these on your graph.
(b) Calculate the residuals and plot them against time.
(iii) Do you think that single exponential smoothing is an effective tool in this case?

Activity

The table below gives the number of tonnes of a particular chemical used each week by a large chemical plant over a period of about 5 years. Use some or all of these data to investigate the performance of exponential smoothing.

Week	Sales	Week	Sales	Week	Sales	Week	Sales	Week	Sales
1	70	53	53	105	57	157	67	209	53
2	80	54	57	106	71	158	46	210	49
3	68	55	74	107	62	159	56	211	49
4	52	56	70	108	52	160	73	212	57
5	37	57	63	109	43	161	54	213	58
6	50	58	56	110	30	162	68	214	88
7	17	59	67	111	39	163	74	215	107

(*continued*)

Activity (continued)

Week	Sales	Week	Sales	Week	Sales	Week	Sales	Week	Sales
8	45	60	50	112	72	164	76	216	98
9	15	61	53	113	63	165	81	217	93
10	38	62	53	114	42	166	78	218	79
11	33	63	60	115	54	167	73	219	75
12	47	64	78	116	44	168	69	220	98
13	48	65	62	117	54	169	56	221	101
14	36	66	68	118	74	170	48	222	105
15	42	67	74	119	66	171	51	223	90
16	43	68	62	120	66	172	50	224	78
17	24	69	53	121	93	173	52	225	67
18	31	70	64	122	74	174	66	226	83
19	32	71	67	123	59	175	74	227	59
20	38	72	60	124	53	176	69	228	49
21	37	73	44	125	52	177	71	229	55
22	54	74	80	126	68	178	74	230	55
23	56	75	79	127	70	179	72	231	78
24	85	76	63	128	74	180	68	232	90
25	77	77	57	129	68	181	61	233	81
26	71	78	72	130	50	182	71	234	63
27	53	79	78	131	50	183	77	235	82
28	55	80	57	132	50	184	66	236	74
29	43	81	61	133	43	185	51	237	74
30	45	82	48	134	61	186	60	238	107
31	75	83	31	135	67	187	49	239	105
32	42	84	59	136	76	188	57	240	85
33	53	85	85	137	64	189	67	241	100
34	51	86	86	138	63	190	39	242	93
35	59	87	73	139	82	191	85	243	106
36	66	88	78	140	71	192	76	244	90
37	76	89	68	141	68	193	73	245	79
38	75	90	83	142	59	194	58	246	67
39	64	91	93	143	42	195	52	247	49
40	55	92	82	144	40	196	34	248	65
41	70	93	68	145	50	197	45	249	57
42	71	94	54	146	34	198	53	250	50
43	84	95	38	147	33	199	59	251	79
44	59	96	37	148	62	200	71	252	74
45	57	97	51	149	91	201	70	253	62
46	68	98	75	150	90	202	72	254	48
47	62	99	63	151	74	203	55	255	39
48	74	100	75	152	41	204	58	256	59
49	62	101	63	153	63	205	51	257	75
50	58	102	85	154	49	206	39	258	89
51	69	103	75	155	52	207	27	259	85
52	57	104	69	156	83	208	21	260	71

KEY POINTS

When you have worked through this chapter you should
- understand the term *autocorrelation*
- understand the effect of autocorrelation on forecasting values in a time series
- be able to interpret a correlogram
- be able to use single exponential smoothing to forecast values in a stationary time series with positive autocorrelation.

Appendix A: Probability plots

Probability plots are an informal means of checking whether a particular probability model is appropriate for a given set of data. They may be used for any distribution but we shall concentrate on the Normal distribution.

Suppose that we have a random sample of size n from a $N(\mu, \sigma^2)$ distribution. We could model this with the random variables

$$X_1, ..., X_n \sim N(\mu, \sigma^2).$$

Then for each of these

$$\frac{X_i - \mu}{\sigma} \sim N(0,1) \qquad (*)$$

We now have n standard Normal random variables. It can be shown that if we take a random sample of size n from a $N(0,1)$ distribution we would expect to get values which would divide the area under the probability density function into approximately $n + 1$ equal parts — just as we would expect a single observation to be near zero and divide the area into two equal parts.

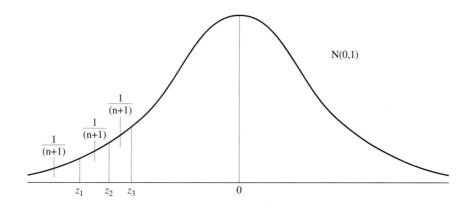

For example, if we had a sample of size 5 from a $N(0,1)$ distribution we would expect the z-values to divide the area under the p.d.f. into six equal parts as shown in the diagram on page 204.

CIS

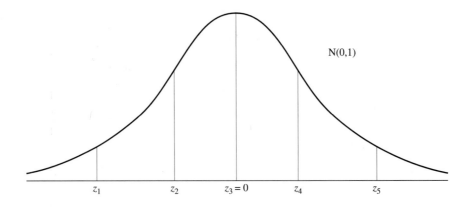

We may find the z-values from the MEI tables.

i	1	2	3	4	5
$\Phi(z_i)$	$1/6 \approx 0.1667$	$2/6 \approx 0.3333$	$3/6 = 0.5$	$4/6 \approx 0.6667$	$5/6 \approx 0.8333$
z_i	-0.9674	-0.4307	0	0.4307	0.9674

If we take our sample of size 5, arrange the values in order and denote them by $x_{(1)}, \ldots, x_{(5)}$ we would expect the smallest standardised value to be approximately -0.9674, the next smallest to be approximately -0.4307, and so on. From the result (*) above we expect

$$\frac{x_{(i)} - \mu}{\sigma} \approx z_i$$

so

$$x_{(i)} \approx \sigma z_i + \mu$$

Comparing this with the standard equation of a line, $y = mx + c$, we see that a plot of $x_{(i)}$ against z_i should be approximately linear with gradient σ and y-intercept μ if the sample is from a $N(\mu, \sigma^2)$ distribution.

When using a probability plot we do not expect the points to lie exactly on a line. If they appear to be randomly scattered about a line we accept that the sample comes from the specified distribution. It is a clear non-linear pattern in the plot which causes us to doubt that the specified distribtuion is a suitable model for the data set.

In the case of Normal probability plots, the following diagrams show the four standard departures from linearity and their causes.

Probability plot				
p.d.f.				
Description	Positively skewed, skewed to the right, like a chi-squared distribution	Negatively skewed, skewed to the left	Less "pointed" than the Normal distribution, like a Student's t-distribution	More "pointed" than a Normal distribution

Most statistical software packages will produce Normal probability plots. For example, in MINITAB the command **nscores c1 c2** will produce the z values corresponding to the x-values in column 1 and put them into column 2. The probability plot is then obtained by plotting column 1 against column 2.

An alternative is to use special "Arithmetic Normal Probability Paper". This has a percentage scale on one axis and the other axis is used to cover the range of the observed values. A percentage cumulative frequency graph is then drawn on the graph paper. As above, a reasonably linear graph supports the use of a Normal distribution to model the data points and a non-linear pattern suggests that the Normal distribution is not a suitable model.

For example, suppose that the values in our sample are as follows.

67.8	67.3	46.9	43.2	59.4	49.3	52.9	60.8	44.7	59.8
64.9	58.5	69.2	56.0	37.9	46.0	58.4	51.3	52.3	38.6

Arranging these in order we have the following.

38.6	39.9	43.2	44.7	46.0	46.9	49.3	51.3	52.3	52.9
56.0	58.4	58.5	59.4	59.8	60.8	64.9	67.3	67.8	69.2

Now, 38.6 is the smallest value of the twenty values, so 5% of the values are less than or equal to 38.6. We plot 38.6 against 5%.

39.9 is the second smallest of the twenty values, so 10% of the values are less than or equal to 39.9. We continue in this way. The final value, 69.2, is not used because the Normal distribution stretches infinitely far over both positive and negative values and so we cannot give a number which will have 100% of the values less than it.

When we plot the values in our sample on arithmetic Normal probability paper we obtain the result shown below.

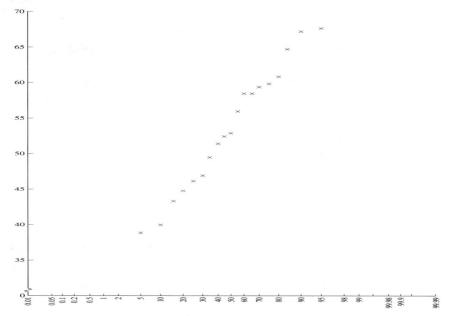

There is a fairly clear S-shaped departure from linearity suggesting that the Normal distribution is not a suitable model.

The first method described may be used for any distribution, continuous or discrete. Special probability paper is available for the Poisson distribution as well as the Normal distribution.

Appendix B:
Testing paired data

The **Wilcoxon Rank Sum Test** (the one sample test, also called, amongst other things, the Wilcoxon Matched Pairs Signed Rank Test) assumes that the two distributions have the same shape and tests whether they have different locations (medians). It uses the ranks of the absolute differences in the values, that is to say, the differences are put in order of size ignoring their signs. In this case there are four values where the absolute difference is 1 and so each is ranked 2.5, which is the mean of the ranks 1, 2, 3 and 4.

Field	A	B	C	D	E	F	G	H	I	J
Difference in yields (new minus standard)	+2	+6	+2	+1	+1	+2	+5	−1	−1	−2
Ranks (+ve bold)	**6.5**	**10**	**6.5**	**2.5**	**2.5**	**6.5**	**9**	2.5	2.5	6.5

The sum of the ranks of those differences which were positive, is $W_+ = 43.5$ and the sum of the ranks of those differences which were negative is $W_- = 11.5$. This may be checked by using the formula $\dfrac{n(n+1)}{2}$ for the sum of the ranks from 1 to n, which gives $\dfrac{10 \times 11}{2} = 55$ in this case and is equal to 43.5 + 11.5. From statistical tables we see that the critical region for a two tailed test at the 5% significance level is $\{W_+ \text{ or } W_- \leq 8\}$ so our results are consistent with the null hypothesis. Again we would say that there is insufficient evidence to conclude that the yield of the new variety is larger than that of the standard variety.

To use a **Student's *t*-Test** we must assume that the differences in the yields come from a Normal distribution. (We could check this using a probability plot, see Appendix A.) Under the null hypothesis the mean of this distribution is zero. We estimate the variance of the distribution from the results and that is why we use a *t*-test rather than a *z*-test.

As usual, the test statistic is

$$t = \frac{\bar{d}}{\sqrt{\dfrac{\hat{\sigma}^2}{10}}} \quad \text{where} \quad \hat{\sigma}^2 = \frac{\sum_{i=1}^{10}(d_i - \bar{d})^2}{9}$$

The critical value for *t* is obtained from statistical tables for a *t*-distribution with nine degrees of freedom, and is 2.262 for a significance level of 5% and a two-tailed test.

CIS

From these results we obtain $\bar{d} = 1.5$ and $\hat{\sigma}^2 = 6.5$ so $t = \dfrac{1.5}{\sqrt{\dfrac{6.5}{10}}} = 1.86$.

Again, the test statistic is not in the critical region so we reach the same conclusion.

Since the different tests involve different assumptions, you may sometimes reach different conclusions depending upon which test is used. Where possible, you need to check the underlying assumptions for each test to ensure that you use the most suitable one for the situation.

Commercial and industrial statistics

Appendix C:
Resistant lines

When we wish to fit a line to a scatter graph, the traditional method is either to fit the line "by eye" or to use the "least squares" regression line. Sometimes we use the fact that the least squares regression line goes through the point $(\bar{x}, \bar{y})$ and therefore calculate the means and then fit the line by eye through that point.

If we use the least squares regression line, there are two problems which occur fairly frequently (both of which are specifically signalled by MINITAB and other statistical software).

The first problem relates to the situation where most of the points lie reasonably close to a line, but one or two points lie a long way above (or below) the line, i.e. the difference is primarily in the value of the y-coordinate. Because the method squares the deviations from any proposed line, these outstanding points have an excessive influence on the position of the line. We could, of course, delete the points but this would probably be too strong a response – unless, upon investigation, we found that they represented errors.

The second problem with the least squares regression method occurs when there is a group of points which are fairly close together and one or two points which are a long way away from the group, i.e. the difference is primarily in the value of the x-coordinate. In this case the outlying points are said to have "high leverage" as the squaring involved means that the line is bound to go through, or very close to, these points. As above, we could delete the points, but this would probably not be appropriate.

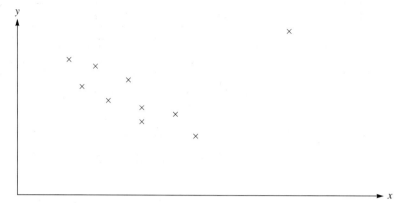

Each of these problems is exacerbated if the number of points involved is small. Even with large data sets, there can still be a significant difference between the least squares regression line found when the outlying points are included and when they are excluded.

Resistant lines are designed to overcome the problems which have been outlined above. The concept is very simple:

1. The data set is divided into three groups, of approximately equal size, with those points with the smallest valued x-coordinates being in the left hand group and those with the largest x-coordinates being in the right hand group.

2. Each group is represented by a "summary point", whose x-coordinate is the median of the values of the x-coordinates of the points in the group, and whose y-coordinate is the median of the y-coordinates of the points in the group.

3. The gradient of the resistant line is given by the gradient of the line joining the summary points for the left hand group and for the right hand group.

4. The y-intercept of the resistant line is the arithmetic mean of the three y-intercepts found when the line of gradient found in (3) is required to go through each of the three summary points.

5. In physical terms, this is equivalent to taking the line joining the left and right summary points and moving it up (or down) one third of the way towards the middle summary point,

There is one further principle which over rides the above:

6. All points with the same x-coordinate **must** go in the same group.

For example, suppose we have the following data giving the levels of two pollutants, in tons per year per km^2, for a former Eastern European country. We want to investigate these to see if there is any association between the two. If there is some association, we would like to be able to forecast the SO_2 level from the NO_x level.

NO$_x$	1.2	0.2	22	0.5	0.7	0.6	0.5	3.8	1.1	0.5	0.6	0.5	2.1
SO$_2$	2.4	1.3	8	0.6	3.8	3.4	3.5	5.9	0.4	1.6	0.6	1.8	1.3

NO$_x$	0.5	2.3	2.2	1.6	1.8	0.4	1.3	0.6	15.7	0.6	1.4	0.9
SO$_2$	2	4.8	2.9	3.5	2.8	0.9	3.5	1.4	5.2	2.2	2.2	1.6

NO$_x$	0.5	0	0.1	0.7	15.8	1.5	1.5	2.2	2.2	0.9	1.5	2.1
SO$_2$	3.2	2	0.7	2.4	2.5	6.3	3.8	4.2	9.4	1.4	3.2	4.3

The first step is, as usual, to plot the data on a scatter graph.

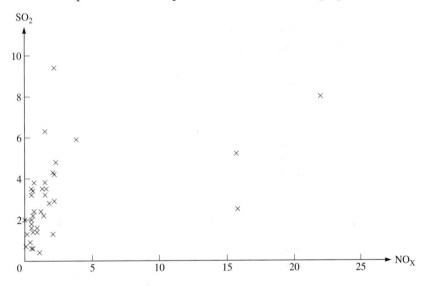

These are correlation data, but we could fit a line for prediction purposes using least squares regression. If we were to do this the three points with NO$_x$ levels exceeding 15 tons per year per km^2 would have a very strong effect on the line. If we were to use a resistant line instead they would still have an effect, but it will not be so large.

1. As there are 37 points, we divide the data into three groups of size 12, 13 and 12 on the basis of the x-coordinates. The values are shown in the table below.

NO$_x$	0	0.1	0.2	0.4	0.5	0.5	0.5	0.5	0.5	0.5	0.6	0.6
SO$_2$	2	0.7	1.3	0.9	0.6	3.5	1.6	1.8	2	3.2	3.4	0.6

NO$_x$	0.6	0.6	0.7	0.7	0.9	0.9	1.1	1.2	1.3	1.4	1.5	1.5	1.5
SO$_2$	1.4	2.2	3.8	2.4	1.6	1.4	0.4	2.4	3.5	2.2	6.3	3.8	3.2

NO$_x$	1.6	1.8	2.1	2.1	2.2	2.2	2.2	2.3	3.8	15.7	15.8	22
SO$_2$	3.5	2.8	1.3	4.3	2.9	4.2	9.4	4.8	5.9	5.2	2.5	8

However, when we do this we find that some points with x-values equal to 0.6 are in the first group and some are in the second. They must all be in the same group. If there were more in one group than in the other we would move them all to the group with the most in originally. In this case there are two in each so we arbitrarily move them all to the first group. The new groups are shown in the table below.

NO_x	0	0.1	0.2	0.4	0.5	0.5	0.5	0.5	0.5	0.5	0.6	0.6	0.6
SO_x	2	0.7	1.3	0.9	0.6	3.5	1.6	1.8	2	3.2	3.4	0.6	1.4

NO_x	0.6	0.7	0.7	0.9	0.9	1.1	1.2	1.3	1.4	1.5	1.5	1.5
SO_x	2.2	3.8	2.4	1.6	1.4	0.4	2.4	3.5	2.2	6.3	3.8	3.2

NO_x	1.6	1.8	2.1	2.1	2.2	2.2	2.2	2.3	3.8	15.7	15.8	22
SO_x	3.5	2.8	1.3	4.3	2.9	4.2	9.4	4.8	5.9	5.2	2.5	8

2.   The summary points are (0.5, 1.7), (1.2, 2.4) and (2.2, 4.25).

Note that within each group, we treat the x-coordinates and the y-coordinate separately, i.e. the x and y values are disassociated from each other.

So, we are now representing our data by the three summary points, as shown below.

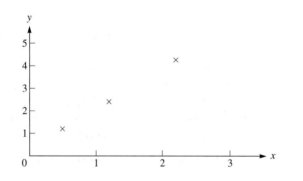

3.   The gradient of the resistant line is given by $\dfrac{4.25 - 1.7}{2.2 - 0.5} = 1.5$

4.   Rearranging the equation $y = mx + c$ to make c the subject, we obtain:

$$c = y - mx$$

Using this, for each of the three summary points we obtain the values 0.95, 0.6 and 0.95 for the y-intercept, c.

Note that the two values obtained using the outer sets are bound to be the same, since we used these to find the gradient of the line.

The y-intercept for the resistant line is the mean of these three values, 0.833…

Thus the equation of our resistant line is

$$y = 1.5x + 0.83$$

and it fits the data as shown below.

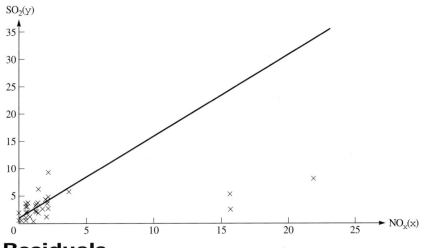

Residuals

As always, we should look at the residuals to see how well our data fit the (linear) model.

Refinement

If the residual plot shows a linear trend we may seek to improve our model (the equation connecting x and y) as follows:

- Find the equation of the resistant line for the residual plot
- Let the new gradient be the sum of the gradients from the original resistant line and the resistant line for the residual plot
- Let the new y-intercept be the sum of the y-intercepts from the original resistant line and the resistant line for the residual plot.

Clearly, we could repeat this procedure several times, if it were appropriate.

Answers to selected exercises

N.B. In quite a number of cases there is no one correct answer — your answer may not be the same as the one given here but may still be correct.

Exercise 1A
1. A simple random sample
2. Random samples selected from each of the three groups of people
3. (a) Not representative   (b) choose the time of each day's sample randomly

Exercise 1B
1. 37 farmers and 263 non-farmers
2. The sample sizes are approximately 175, 233, 247 and 34 to the nearest whole number

Exercise 1C
1. Cluster sample   **2.** Stratified sample   **3.** Stratify on the number of people in the home

Exercise 1D
1. (i)(b) 43   68   81   06   11   88   26   37   09   23   77   16   44   14   74   39   12   01   64   05

Exercise 2A
1. About $\pm 4.5\%$ **2.** 300   **3.** 400
4. Using the 10% estimate, 3600; using a conservative estimate, 10 000
5. About 2.25%   **6.** (i) Between 4% and 24%   (ii) Between 800 and 4800
7. 10 000 (he probably needs to accept less precision)

Exercise 2B
1. (ii) About £3248 to £261 000
2.

Area	A	B	C
(i)(a) mean, $\bar{x}$	5080	15 180	29 780
(i)(b) s.d., $\hat{\sigma}$	1718.328...	3055.206...	5826.715...
(iii) & (iv) $\bar{x} + 3\hat{\sigma}$	10 235	24 348	47 260

(v) A single policy does not seem like a good idea, but a single policy for each of the areas might work
3. About 1290kg to 1460kg

Exercise 2C
1. Point estimate for the proportion is about 19% and the interval is from 175 to 21%; point estimate for the time since purchase/upgrade is just over 3 years and the interval is from just under 3 years to about 3 years and 3 months
2. 3600
4. (i) It guarantees that almost the whole range is covered
   (ii) Roughly from £3300 to £3900
   (iii) Use a scatter plot to look for a relationship
5. Estimate of total issue readership is 64 280 and of total weekly readership is 85 340
6. (i) Sample sizes 20, 23, 20, 17, 8, 6,7 (total 101)   (ii) 52884.8
7. (i) 314 346 ha   (ii) About 10% which could have a large effect

Exercise 2D
1. 7/8 and from 0.7 to 1
2. $n = 500$

p

θ		0.1	0.2	0.3	0.4	0.5	0.6	0.7	0.8	0.9
	0.1	0.0005	0.0006	0.0007	0.0008	0.0008	0.0008	0.0007	0.0006	0.0005
	0.2	0.0011	0.0012	0.0013	0.0014	0.0014	0.0014	0.0013	0.0012	0.0011
	0.3	0.0028	0.0029	0.0030	0.0031	0.0031	0.0031	0.0030	0.0029	0.0028
	0.4	0.0122	0.0123	0.0124	0.0125	0.0125	0.0125	0.0124	0.0123	0.0122

The results are symmetrical about $p = 0.05$; the variance increases as p and/or θ approaches 0.5
3. (i) 9/150 or 18%; from 0 to 37%   (ii) 18% again; from 12% to 24%
4. 21%; from 0% to 43%

Exercise 3B
2. Data support the claim of a 25% reduction   **4.** –2.18, reject NH
5. (i) Due to chance   (ii) profit rather than yield

Exercise 3D
1. The values in the table below are given to 2 decimal places. Your values might differ slightly.

		Fertiliser				
		P	Q	R	T	Field effects
	A	3.96	2.39	–1.32	–5.04	–19.82
	B	2.96	–0.61	1.68	–4.04	–12.82
Field	C	0.71	1.14	–1.57	–0.29	–6.57
(Block)	D	3.96	–2.61	–3.32	1.96	0.18
	E	–3.54	–0.11	3.18	0.46	7.68
	F	–3.29	–0.86	1.43	2.71	13.43
	G	–4.79	0.64	–0.07	4.21	17.93
	Treatment effects	–17.46	–5.89	4.82	18.54	81.32

All seem to represent real effects
2.

		Variety				
		Haven	Hereward	Hunter	Riband	Block effects
	1	–200	400	–240	40	20
	2	250	–50	–90	–110	170
Block	3	50	–250	110	90	170
	4	–100	0	160	–60	20
	5	0	–100	60	40	–380
	Variety effects	100	300	–260	–140	7580

Differences between the varieties seem to be real effects apart from the difference between Hunter and Riband
3. Case 1: the results of median pollish are given in the table below

		Machine			
		A	B	C	Worker effect
	P	5	0	–3	15
	Q	0	0	–4	25
Worker	R	7	0	0	0
	S	0	0	2	–8
	T	–1	0	1	–10
	Machine effect	–7	0	8	59

It is likely that the differences are real

		Machine			
		A	B	C	Worker effect
	P	9	0	–6	12
	Q	0	13	–5	16
Worker	R	1	–12	0	0
	S	–16	0	8	–11
	T	–13	0	14	–13
	Machine effect	–1	0	5	62

Differences between the machines could well be due to chance

4. (i)

Pattern of application

		X	Y	Z	Block effect
Block	1	0	0	0	500
	2	−200	0	0	400
	3	0	200	−300	0
	4	200	0	300	−100
	5	−400	400	−300	0
	Application effect	−200	0	300	8000

(ii) Differences between the patterns could have occurred by chance

Pattern of application

		X	Y	Z	Block effect
Block	1	0	0	100	−100
	2	−200	0	−100	400
	3	300	−100	100	100
	4	300	0	0	0
	5	0	700	−400	−200
	Application effect	−300	0	400	7500

All differences could be due to chance

5. Sweeping by means we obtain the following results

		Natural	High	Low	Block effect
Pen block	1	2.58	2.08	−4.67	20.92
	2	−7.42	2.08	5.33	−11.08
	3	−15.75	−10.25	26	4.25
	4	20.58	6.08	−26.67	−14.08
	Treatment effect	−26.25	16.25	10	332.75

When compared with the size of the residuals, there seems to be a fairly clear increase in the number of eggs laid when using the extensions to the natural day. However, the difference between the two forms of lighting for extending the day could well be due to chance variation.

6. (ii)

Machine

		1	2	3	4	5	Product effect
Product	A	8	0	7	−8	−7	2
	B	7	0	7	−8	−6	−7
	C	0	0	−5	4	7	−4
	D	−3	0	−9	1	6	0
	E	5	0	0	0	0	0
	Machine effect	−10	−10	5	0	1	31

Exercise 3E

1. (a) Cross-over design   (b) Cross-over design   (c) Cross-over design   (d) Cross-over design

2. (i) Buy machine P, but not significant at the 5% level

Exercise 4A

1.

Operator

		A	B	C	D	Batch effect
Fabric type	1	3.5	2.75	−0.5	−5.75	−25
	2	−0.75	−2	−1.75	4.5	−14.25
	3	−1	2.25	−2	0.75	24
	4	−1.75	−3	4.25	0.5	15.25
	Operator effect	−40.75	−18	8.75	50	1114.75

Machine	1	2	3	4
Machine effect	−148.5	−51.5	49	151

From the size of the residuals, the differences between machines are probably real. Machines improve from 1 to 4

2. Finding the means gives the following results

Cow

	P	Q	R	S	Period effect
1	−7.25	3.25	3.5	0.5	17.375
2	−3	−0.75	3	0.75	2.125
3	3	4.75	−7	−0.75	−6.125
4	7.25	−7.25	0.5	0.5	−13.375
	1.875	−16.625	21.875	−7.125	114.375

Diet	A	B	C	D
Diet effect	−17.375	−7.375	8.875	15.875

The diet appears to increase in effect from A to D. Both C and D are better than A and B but other differences could be due to chance.

3. After sweeping by means we obtain the following results

Variety

		Haven	Hereward	Riband	Field effects
	1	−200	266.7	−66.7	−33.3
	2	266.7	−66.7	−200	133.3
Field	3	−66.7	−200	266.7	−100
	Variety effect	−33.3	166.7	−133.3	7633.3

Pattern	X	Y	Z
Effect	100	33.33333	−133.333

The residuals are large compared with the pattern effects after attempting to fit the additive model, so it looks as though the differences could just be due to chance variation. If, instead, we use medians, we obtain the same results (with different numbers in the table)

Exercise 4B

2. Mean effect of A over a is 21.5; mean effect of B over b is −5; mean effect of C over c is +2; interaction between A and B is −3; interaction between A and C is −25; interaction between B and C is +4
3. Representing catalyst by a, temperature by b, and additive by c, the mean effect of A over a is 0; mean effect of B over b is 11.5; mean effect of C over c is 0; interaction between A and B is −50; interaction between A and C is +1; interaction between B and C is +2
4. A standard 2^3 factorial experiment, with replications if possible
5. (ii) Mean effect of A over a is −13.5; mean effect of B over b is +6; mean effect of C over c is −33; interaction between A and B is −5; interaction between A and C is +3; interaction between B and C is −2
  (iii) 104.5

Exercise 5B

3. Sample of size 50
4. Reject loads when there are 6 or more substandard plants in a sample of 50

Exercise 5C

2. (iii) 6.1., 69.7 and 80.9
3. (i) 0.982   (ii) 0.9927   (iii) 4.615
  (iv) if $p = 0.01$ is an acceptable level of defectives then the double sampling scheme is to be preferred as there is a higher probability of accepting such a batch (0.99 as opposed to 0.98) and a smaller number of items is inspected (4.23 on average instead of 20)

Exercise 6A

1. $t = 3$ no action; $t = 5$ no action; $t = 6$ stop the process; $t = 8$ no action; $t = 10$ stop the process

CIS

2. Warning lines at 25.228 and 25.252; action lines at 25.222 and 25.258. The process should have been stopped following the samples taken at 9:15, 11:15 and 14:15

Exercise 6B

1. 5/3 **2.** 0.77 **4.** Start when centred on 60.02 mm and stop when centred on 59.98 mm

Exercise 6C

1. Warning limits 0.0087 mm and 0.00579 mm; action limits 0.0003 mm and 0.00774 mm
2. (i) Estimate of the standard deviation = 2.8796 to 4 d.p.; warning limits for the mean are 97.42 and 102.58; action limits for the mean are 96.14 and 103.86; warning limits for the range are 2.37 and 11.58; action limits for the range are 1.02 and 15.1
(ii) Both charts suggest that the process is well in (statistical) control; the process should have been stopped after sample 4 because of the means and after sample 8 because of the ranges

Exercise 6D

1. (i) Standard deviation 0.01, warning lines for the mean are 2.491 and 2.509 and the action lines are 0.00088 and 0.01298

Exercise 6E

1. (i) Sample 14 (ii) No cause for concern
2. Polymerisation time batch 17; vacuum time batch 20

Exercise 6F

1. The warning limits are $11.6 \pm 2\sqrt{11.2636}$ which gives 4.88... and 18.31... (proportions 0.0122 and 0.0458); the

action limits are $11.6 \pm \sqrt{11.2636}$ which gives 1.53... and 21.66... (proportions 0.0038 and 0.0542)
2. (i) Warning line between 4 and 5; action line between 6 and 7

3. Warning limits are $3.1 \pm 3\sqrt{3.2}$ which are −0.42 and 6.62 so there is no lower warning limit; upper warning

limit is between 6 and 7; upper action limit is $3.1 + 3\sqrt{3.1}$ which is 8.38... so it is set between 8 and 9.

4. Warning limits are $14.6 \pm \sqrt{14.6} = 6.95...$ and 22.24...; action limits are $14.6 \pm 3\sqrt{14.6} = 3.13...$ and 26.06; the process should have been stopped after sample 14. The values seem to be higher than would be expected if the mean were 14.6

Exercise 8B

1. 10929; these forecasts cannot be expected to be at all reliable
2. Estimate for Jan 1996 is 10.71; estimate for Feb 1996 is 9.61
3. The trend line is $y = 528.3475t + 83554.45$; the estimate for the first quarter of 1996 is 89141.73 which should probably be given as 89100, or from 88600 to 89600

Exercise 8C
1. (i) 1 (ii) 0 **2.** (i) 0.8 (ii) 0.96

Exercise 9A
2. From 4229 to 4248; from 4227 to 4249; from 4224 to 4253 **3.** 2436.29

Exercise 10A
1.

Lag	1	2	3	4
Correlation	−0.0828	0.827	−0.688	0.588

2.

Lag	1	2	3	4
Correlation	−0.501	−0.102	0.276	−0.423

Exercise 10B

1. (i)(b) Values are positively autocorrelated

Index